A Literary Guide to Washington, DC

A Literary Guide
TO
Washington, DC

Walking in the Footsteps of
American Writers from
Francis Scott Key to
Zora Neale Hurston

KIM ROBERTS

University of Virginia Press
CHARLOTTESVILLE AND LONDON

University of Virginia Press
© 2018 by the Rector and Visitors of the University of Virginia
All rights reserved
Printed in the United States of America on acid-free paper

First published 2018

9 8 7 6 5 4 3 2 1

Library of Congress Cataloging-in-Publication Data
Names: Roberts, Kim, 1961– author.
Title: A literary guide to Washington, DC : walking in the footsteps
of American writers from Francis Scott Key to Zora Neale Hurston /
Kim Roberts.
Description: Charlottesville : University of Virginia Press, 2018. |
Includes bibliographical references and index.
Identifiers: LCCN 2017059448 | ISBN 9780813941165 (cloth : alk. paper) |
ISBN 9780813941172 (pbk. : alk. paper) | ISBN 9780813941189 (e-book)
Subjects: LCSH: American literature Bio-bibliography.—Washington
(D.C.) | Authors, American—Homes and haunts—Washington (D.C.)—
Guidebooks. | Literary landmarks—Washington (D.C.)—Guidebooks. |
Washington (D.C.)—Intellectual life. | Washington (D.C.)—Guidebooks.
Classification: LCC PS144.W18 L58 2018 | DDC 810.9/9753—dc23
LC record available at https://lccn.loc.gov/2017059448

Cover art: Dunbar House, Adams Memorial, and Smithsonian National
Portrait Gallery photographed by Dan Vera; photos of Walt Whitman,
Zora Neale Hurston, Langston Hughes, and Frances Hodgson Burnett
and 1792 plan of the city of Washington courtesy of the Library of
Congress, Prints and Photographs Division

For Dan Vera
Hic manebimus optime

Contents

Acknowledgments   ix

Introduction   3

Beginnings, 1800–1861

Portraits
Joel Barlow   11
Francis Scott Key   13
Michael G. Shiner   17
Anne Lynch Botta   23

The Civil War Era, 1861–1865

Walking Tour 1: Walt Whitman's Downtown   29

Portraits
John Burroughs   54
Solomon G. Brown   59
Charlotte Forten Grimké   68

Reconstruction, 1865–1878

Walking Tour 2: Paul Laurence Dunbar and
Alice Dunbar-Nelson in LeDroit Park   75

Portraits
Frederick Douglass   105
Frances Hodgson Burnett   111

The Gilded Age, 1870–1910

Walking Tour 3: Henry Adams in
Lafayette Square   119

Portraits
Mark Twain   146
Ambrose Bierce   149
Elinor Wylie   152

The Jazz Age, 1920–1930

Walking Tour 4: Langston Hughes and the
Harlem Renaissance along U Street   159

Portraits
Georgia Douglas Johnson   192
Sinclair Lewis   198
Jean Toomer   201
Zora Neale Hurston   203

Selected Bibliography   209
Index   221

Acknowledgments

First and foremost, I thank two dear friends without whom this book would never have been written: Dan Vera and Martin G. Murray. Their careful scholarship and wit has been an inspiration, and a model I have striven to emulate.

Other scholars researching the history of Washington, DC, have also been instrumental in my thinking, and I thank especially Michon Boston, Patsy Fletcher, Brian Gilmore, Marya Annette McQuirter, Peter Montgomery, and Myra Sklarew.

The walking tours in this book were developed over the span of nearly twenty years, and several groups and individuals were instrumental in providing crucial information, material support, and on-the-ground audiences for earlier drafts. I thank, in particular, Humanities DC (especially Joy Ford Austin and Jasper Collier), the Washingtoniana Collection at the DC Public Library, the annual DC Historical Studies Conference, Split This Rock Poetry Festival (and Sarah Browning), the Cornell Club of Washington (and Linda Jarschauer Johnson), the Moorland-Spingarn Collection at Howard University, the Word Works, Inc. (and Karren LaLonde Alenier), the Kiplinger Library at the Historical Society of Washington, the Folger Shakespeare Library (and Teri Ellen Cross Davis), the Sumner School Museum and Archives (and Kimberly Springle), the continuing education program at Cedar Lane Unitarian Church, and the Gelman Library Special Collections at the George Washington University (and Jennifer King).

A different version of walking tour 1, which covers some of the same sites, was cowritten with Martin G. Murray and published by the Rainbow History Project as part of their "Gay DC Walking Tours" brochure series in 2005. I am indebted to Martin for his fine research and this collaboration.

At the University of Virginia Press, I am indebted to my editor, Eric Brandt, for his belief in this project. Most of the historical photos in this book are used courtesy of the Library of Congress—what would I do without that peerless national resource? The contemporary photos were provided thanks (again) to the indefatigable Dan Vera. And the beautiful maps were created by Nat Case of INCase, LLC.

Finally, I want to acknowledge my family. The memory of my maternal grandmother, Tessie Oberstein Berwick, is a blessing. My love also goes out to my brother, Kenneth Berwick Roberts, and sister-in-law, Sally Smith Roberts, and to my nephews and nieces: Aaron Berwick Roberts and Hillary Jones Roberts, and Lizzie Roberts Wong and Silas Wong.

A Literary Guide to Washington, DC

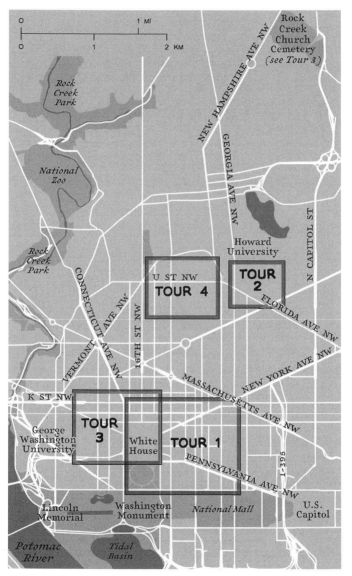

Washington, DC

Introduction

This book tells the story of Washington, DC's writers, from the founding of the city through the beginnings of modernism, covering the period from roughly 1800 through 1930. It combines walking tours focused on an area's most prominent writers with brief portraits of individual writers of note. Some of these writers will be familiar to any well-read American; many will, I hope, be new discoveries.

Writers have always been drawn to the nation's capital city, to work for the government, to cover governmental affairs for newspapers, and simply to be in close proximity to power. Other institutions have also attracted writers: schools and universities, museums (notably the Smithsonian Institution), embassies, news outlets, and the vast network of businesses and organizations that support and serve the federal presence. Since the founding of Washington, DC, its writers have interpreted and documented the culture of the city, joining in a larger American conversation. As we read, we tap into ancestral voices that have shaped our landscape, deepening our sense of place.

The city of Washington is elastic enough to accept tribute along with harsh criticism. It is a rich landscape and a forgiving one. With all the congressional grandstanding, abuses of power large and small, and the pure idealism that keeps workers entering federal service, the city's literary community has kept its parallel path.

This book is organized into five parts, corresponding to five (sometimes overlapping) time periods that mark the most ferment in the city's early literary communities. In its nascent antebellum period, DC was a small town with few year-round residents and a seasonal influx of part-timers who swelled their ranks each winter, when Congress was in session. But even in that early era, there was a sense of larger purpose, a shared feeling that the capital city could be a national model, that its broad avenues could symbolize democracy—although from the start, democracy was meted out unevenly.

In the city's earliest years, prior to the Civil War, significant writers included Joel Barlow, a diplomat most famous for negotiating a treaty with Napoléon Bonaparte and the Treaty of Tripoli; Daniel Webster, renowned orator, congressman, senator, and secretary of state; Francis Scott Key, who penned the lyrics to the national anthem; Paul Jennings, who wrote the first slave memoir about serving in the White House; and Josiah Henson, author of two memoirs and the model for Uncle Tom in Harriet Beecher Stowe's novel *Uncle Tom's Cabin* (1852).

During the Civil War era, DC was the center of the war for the Union. Walt Whitman came to the city to volunteer in the many war hospitals, as did other writers: Clara Barton, Louisa May Alcott, Amanda Akin Stearns, Jane Stuart Woolsey. The city's population exploded: according to the U.S. Census Bureau, in 1810 the population was slightly less than 15,500; by 1870 it had grown to 131,700. The expansion of the government brought such writers as John James Piatt (along with his more talented wife, Sarah Morgan Bryan Piatt), William Douglas O'Connor, John Burroughs, John Willis Menard, Charlotte Forten Grimké, and John Hay, among others. Journalists who covered the war from DC included Lawrence A. Gobright, Thomas Bailey Aldrich, Howard Glyndon (pen name for the remarkable Laura Redden Searing, who was deaf), and George Alfred Townsend, better known as Gath. The Civil War marks DC's transition from a small town to a major city.

Even before the Civil War's end, DC began to attract a large African American population whose intellectuals and writers were drawn to, and often affiliated with, educational institutions such as Howard University, M Street High School, the Association for the Study of Negro Life and History, and the American Negro Academy. DC's community of intellectuals of color would become one of the most prominent in the nation. Writers who lived in DC during Reconstruction make an eminent list: Frederick Douglass, Elizabeth Keckley, Alexander Crummell, Mary Ann Shadd Cary, Solomon G. Brown, Anna Julia Cooper, Kelly Miller, Mary Church Terrell, James Weldon Johnson, Alice Dunbar-Nelson, and Paul Laurence Dunbar among them.

As the city continued a rapid expansion through World War I and the Jazz Age, the number of writers grew as well, bringing to DC some of the nation's writers at the forefront of modernist movement. This list includes the first American to win the Nobel Prize in Literature, Sinclair Lewis, and such luminaries of the Harlem Renaissance period as Langston Hughes and Zora Neale Hurston.

Many reformers sought to start national movements in the capital city, using Washington as a proving ground. Hence, slavery was outlawed in 1862 in the District, nine months before Lincoln signed the Emancipation Proclamation (and it was the only place in the United States where slave owners were given monetary compensation for emancipating their slaves). Universal manhood suffrage was granted in DC in 1866, prior to passage of the Fifteenth Amendment to the

Constitution. The first high school for African Americans was founded here in 1870. Prohibition started in DC in 1917, two full years prior to the passage of the Eighteenth Amendment that made it the law across the United States.

This sense that DC should act as a "model city" for the nation affected its writers as well. From the start, literary communities in the city saw themselves as having a special status based on their location. DC's writers have always included presidents, statesmen, lawyers, foreign diplomats, and other people in prominent positions.

But this has worked against writers living in the shadow of the Capitol as well. Unlike many major U.S. cities, such as New York, Chicago, and Boston, DC has never had the reputation as a great city for the arts. Writers, like other artists here, have an underdog status. At times, that has encouraged an enhanced sense of community, as writers have banded together for mutual support. But, especially in the city's early years, it has also meant that there have been fewer bookstores, publishing houses, and theaters than in other cities of comparable size. Writers have struggled for recognition among the throngs of politicians.

The idea that government is DC's only business is pervasive among outsiders. Those who have lived here have always known differently. This book celebrates a wide range of authors who made their living in the capital in different ways as the city grew and modernized. By examining the city's early history, I have tried to make DC's least-well-understood periods more accessible.

Contemporary writers are indebted to the writers who have come before, and learning about them makes all of us better readers, as well as better citizens. The early literature of the capital city, fascinating in itself, reveals much about its time and place and forms a basis for understanding the city today. Walking in the footsteps of our literary forebears connects us in a tangible way to our influences and history. And these important early writers provide a literary genealogy from which contemporary writers and readers continue to draw.

Beginnings,
1800–1861

Portraits

Joel Barlow

March 24, 1754–December 26, 1812

Joel Barlow was a career diplomat whose most significant accomplishments were brokering a commercial treaty with Napoléon Bonaparte when he was American plenipotentiary to France and the negotiation of the Tripoli Treaty (1796) while serving as American consul to Algiers, which protected U.S. ships from piracy (and which contained the controversial phrase that "the Government of the United States of America is not, in any sense, founded on the Christian religion").

Barlow served in the Revolutionary War in the Battle of Long Island. After his graduation from Yale College in 1778, Barlow moved to Hartford, Connecticut, where he became a journalist, passed the bar, and became associated with a group of writers known as the "Hartford Wits," known for their satirical political writings. He began his diplomatic career in 1795.

Barlow's books of poems are *The Vision of Columbus* (1787), *Conspiracy of Kings* (1792), *The Hasty-Pudding* (1793), and *The Columbiad* (1807). He also published essays and political commentary.

From 1805 to 1811, Barlow lived in DC with his wife, Ruth, on an estate he named Kalorama (now the site of both the embassy of Myanmar and the historic Myers House on S Street NW). They owned the largest private library in the city, and their home became a gathering place for the city's cultural elite. The mansion, which stood long enough to serve as a Civil War hospital,

Joel Barlow

was razed in 1888, but the surrounding neighborhood retains the name (and the "beautiful view" which inspired it).

Barlow is buried in Poland, where he died on his last diplomatic assignment, in the village of Zarnowiec, west of Krakow. An American career diplomat restored his plaque in the Zarnowiec Parish Church in 1996.

FROM THE COLUMBIAD

. . . Resplendent o'er the rest, the regent god
Potowmak towers, and sways the swelling flood;
Vines clothe his arms, wild fruits o'erfill his horn,
Wreaths of green maize his reverend brows adorn,

His silver beard reflects the lunar day,
And round his loins the scaly nations play.
. . . .
Then shall your federal towers my bank adorn,
And hail with me the great millennial morn
That gilds your capitol. Thence earth shall draw
Her first clear codes of liberty and law;
There public right a settled form shall find,
Truth trim her lamp to lighten humankind,
Old Afric's sons their shameful fetters cast,
Our wild Hesperians humanize at last,
All men participate, all time expand
The source of good my liberal sages plann'd.
. . . .
In this mid site, this monumental clime,
Rear'd by all realms to brave the wrecks of time
A spacious dome swells up, commodious great,
The last resort, the unchanging scene of state.
On rocks of adamant the walls ascend,
Tall columns heave and sky-like arches bend;
Bright o'er the golden roofs the glittering spires
Far in the concave meet the solar fires;
Four blazing fronts, with gates unfolding high,
Look with immortal splendor round the sky:
Hither the delegated sires ascend,
And all the cares of every clime attend.

Francis Scott Key

August 1, 1779–January 11, 1843

A lawyer, Francis Scott Key is best known as the person who wrote the lyrics to the U.S. national anthem, "The Star Spangled Banner." That poem (printed here under its original title) was written after Key witnessed the

Francis Scott Key

bombing of Fort McHenry during the Battle of Baltimore in the War of 1812; it was set to the tune of a popular British drinking song, "To Anacreon in Heaven."

In addition to occasional poems (collected into a
book that was published fourteen years after his death),
Key published a nonfiction book, *The Power of Literature, and Its Connection with Religion* (1834). Key lived at
The Maples, 619 D Street SE on Capitol Hill from 1815
through 1838. That property is listed on the Register
of Historic Places. He later moved to 3516–18 M Street
NW in Georgetown, now razed, but once preserved as a
museum to the author.

Key is remembered locally by a bridge named in his
honor, linking the Georgetown neighborhood where he

once lived with the Rosslyn neighborhood in Arlington, Virginia. A park on the DC side includes a bust of the author. In addition, Key Elementary School, part of the DC Public School system, and Key Halls at the George Washington University and at the University of Maryland at College Park are named for him. He is buried in Mt. Olivet Cemetery in Frederick, Maryland, in a crypt underneath a monument topped with a bronze sculpture of Key.

DEFENSE OF FORT M'HENRY

O say can you see, by the dawn's early light,
What so proudly we hail'd at the twilight's last gleaming,
Whose broad stripes and bright stars through the perilous
    fight
O'er the ramparts we watch'd were so gallantly streaming?
And the rocket's red glare, the bombs bursting in air,
Gave proof through the night that our flag was still there,
O say does that star-spangled banner yet wave
O'er the land of the free and the home of the brave?

On the shore dimly seen through the mists of the deep
Where the foe's haughty host in dread silence reposes,
What is that which the breeze, o'er the towering steep,
As it fitfully blows, half conceals, half discloses?
Now it catches the gleam of the morning's first beam,
In full glory reflected now shines in the stream,
'Tis the star-spangled banner—O long may it wave
O'er the land of the free and the home of the brave!

And where is that band who so vauntingly swore,
That the havoc of war and the battle's confusion
A home and a Country should leave us no more?
Their blood has wash'd out their foul footstep's pollution.
No refuge could save the hireling and slave

From the terror of flight or the gloom of the grave,
And the star-spangled banner in triumph doth wave
O'er the land of the free and the home of the brave.

O thus be it ever when freemen shall stand
Between their lov'd home and the war's desolation!
Blest with vict'ry and peace may the heav'n rescued land
Praise the power that hath made and preserv'd us a nation!
Then conquer we must, when our cause it is just,
And this be our motto—"In God is our trust,"
And the star-spangled banner in triumph shall wave
O'er the land of the free and the home of the brave.

TO MY COUSIN MARY

For Mending My Tobacco Pouch

Thy stitches are not "few and far between,"
As other stitches very often are,
And many things beside, as I have seen,
In this sad world where good things are so rare;
But they are even, neat, and close enough
My treasured sweets to hold in purest plight;
To keep tobacco safe, and even snuff,
And thus at once eyes, nose, and mouth delight.

They're like thy smiles, fair cousin, frequent, bright,
And ever bringing pleasure in their train;
They're like thy teeth of pearl, and their pure white,
Like them, shall never know tobacco's stain.
Then let me view my stores, and all the while
Look on thy stitches, thinking on thy smile—
But ah! those smiles in distance far are hid,
But here the stitches are—and I will take a quid.

Michael G. Shiner

1805–January 17, 1880

Michael Shiner spent his early years as a farm laborer, enslaved to William Pumphrey of Maryland. Sometime around 1812 or 1813, he was brought to DC. In 1828, Michael Shiner was sold to Thomas Howard Sr., then the chief clerk of the Washington Navy Yard. Howard leased out his slave to the Navy Yard paint shop, where, over the next decade, Shiner learned his trade.

A provision of Pumphrey's will stipulated that Shiner be manumitted after serving fifteen years as a "term slave." Howard's will also noted this provision, reiterating that Shiner be manumitted in eight more years. But Shiner had to sue for his freedom: he filed a petition with the DC Circuit Court in 1836 to force the Howard family to honor the terms of the wills and release him from bondage. The Howard family was served a summons and conceded his freedom. As Shiner wrote, "The only master I have now is the Constitution."

Once freed, Shiner continued his Navy Yard employment, invested in real estate (in today's Ward 6), and took an active role in local Republican Party politics. His final job, at age seventy, was as a police officer assigned to Eastern Market. His *Diary,* the earliest known by a DC resident of African descent, covers the years 1813 to 1869. He married Phillis, a slave owned by William Pumphrey's brother James, around 1828. Shiner was able to purchase the freedom of his wife and three children just in time to prevent their sale to the Deep South.

Shiner learned to read and write in the Sabbath School at Israel Bethel Colored Methodist Episcopal Church, located on Capitol Hill. That congregation, founded by workers of color employed at the Navy Yard, met in temporary quarters until purchasing the church (formerly the First Presbyterian Church of Washington). Israel Bethel and Union Bethel later merged, becoming Metropolitan African Methodist Episcopal Church, now located at 1518 M Street NW, and the oldest continuously operating black church in DC.

Shiner's *Diary* gives a firsthand account of the War of 1812 and several notable events at the Washington Navy Yard and in the city. The manuscript was acquired by the Library of Congress sometime after 1905. In 2007, the book was completely transcribed and edited by John G. Sharp. This remarkable journal reflects Shiner's interest in DC's public events, his religious conviction, and his patriotism. I have regularized his spelling, grammar, and punctuation in the following two excerpts.

In 1833, Shiner rescued his family from the notorious Franklin and Armfield slave jail. Franklin and Armfield's offices were located at 1315 Duke Street in Alexandria, Virginia. Now known as the Freedom House Museum, the building was designated a National Historic Landmark in 1978 and is now administered by the Northern Virginia Urban League. Franklin and Armfield were the largest domestic slave dealers in the United States from 1828 to 1836, notorious for shipping up to 1,200 slaves annually from the Mid-Atlantic to the Deep South. Had Shiner's family been sold, they would have been marched overland in a chained coffle to a slave market outside Natchez, Mississippi, where they would have been sold individually to the highest bidders.

Shiner was able to call upon some powerful allies at the Washington Navy Yard, who knew him as a loyal employee:

The fifth day of June 1833, on Wednesday, my wife and children Phillis Shiner were sold to a couple of gentlemen, Mr. Franklin and Mr. John Armfield, and were carried down to Alexandria. On the sixth day of June 1833 on Thursday, and the seventh day of June 1833 on Friday, I went to Alexandria three times in one day over the Long Bridge and I was in great distress. But nevertheless with the assistance of God I got my wife and children clear. . . .

I am under ten thousand obligations to the Honorable Major General Hamlin for his kindness to me and my wife and children. On the seventh day of June 1833 on Friday, the General laid a detachment on my wife and three children at Mr. Armfield's Jail and took them from there, and put them in the county jail of Alexandria to wait action of the court; and my wife and children remained in the county jail in Alexandria from the seventh of June 1833 until the eleventh of June 1833 on Tuesday, and the same day Mr. Levy Pumphrey executed papers and manumitted them free. The papers were executed at the City Hall in Washington. She came up from Alexandria on the twelfth day of June 1833 on Wednesday. And I am also under obligations to Mr. Steil and Mrs. Steil for their kindness to my wife and children while they were in the jail, and may the Almighty bless them. They gave me such a race at that time that all the people that were acquainted with the affair in Alexandria were sorry for me and appeared to be willing to relieve me of my distress.

I am under great obligation to Commodore Isaac Hull for the time my wife was sold to George. He had command of the Washington Navy Yard. For his kindness to me, and also to Captain John H. Aulic for his kindness too when my wife was sold to George, and also to Captain Joseph Hull for his kindness to me at that time. He was First Lieutenant of the Washington Navy Yard. And also under the same obligation to Major Cary Seldon who was Naval Store Keeper and also to Mr. John Etheridge who at that time was Commodore's Clerk and also to David Eaton, boatswain.

All those above named gentlemen, all of them were willing to help me out of my distresses in an honest, upright way when my wife and children were snatched away from me and sold on the fifth day of June 1833 on Wednesday, from near West Alley between Seventh and Eighth Streets East. May the Lord Bless them all; I shall never forget them.

The Snow Storm was DC's first race riot. It was begun in August 1835 with an alleged nighttime attack by Arthur Bowen, a nineteen-year-old slave, upon his owner, Anna Maria Thornton, aged sixty, widow of the architect of the Capitol, William Thornton. Thornton was then living in a row house on F Street NW (later numbered 1331 F, now the site of an office tower). She called her neighbors for help in calming Bowen, who was drunk when he entered her bedroom with an ax (which she later swore he never raised). Although this sounds highly suspicious, modern readers must remember that axes were common items in every household at that time, as wood was used to heat homes, and Bowen claimed this ax had fallen down in the front hall, tripping him, and that he picked it up in order to find a better place for it.

Nevertheless, knowing he was accused of something very serious, Bowen fled. After three days, he returned home and was arrested and imprisoned in the city jail in today's Judiciary Square. A crowd soon gathered, consisting primarily of white laborers (or, as they were known at the time, "mechanics"), mostly Irish immigrants who were poor, had little or no job security, and had to compete against free African Americans and slaves for work.

Shiner wrote:

On the seventh of August 1835, on Friday, it was reported that Mrs. Doctor Thornton's young mulatto man said that he was going to knock his mistress in the head with an axe, and he was arrested and put in the jail. Still the mob raged with great vigor, and as fast as they were arrested they were lodged in jail. On the eighth day of August 1835, on Saturday, the mob surrounded the jail and swore they would pull the jail down and the Constable was making threats. They said their object was to get Mrs. Thornton's mulatto man out and to hang him without judge or juror. And every effort was made by the Marshal of the District and the United States District Attorney, lawyer Frances Key Sr., and the Honorable William A. Bradley, who was Mayor of Washington at that time. Every effort was made by the officers to preserve peace and harmony among these men but all of it appeared in vain, and there was not sufficient military force to guard the jail, and orders came down from the Navy Department to Lieutenant Colonel Henderson who was at that time Lieutenant Colonel of the Marine Corps, by the Honorable Secretary of the Navy, Levy Wood Berry, to send a detachment of United States Marines without delay to guard the United States Jail in Washington. And Lieutenant Colonel Henderson complied speedily; the Marines went up to the jail on the eighth of August 1835, on Saturday, and they did their duty without faction or favor.

As Shiner reports, Francis Scott Key, then serving as DC's district attorney, called in a detachment of U.S. Marines from the Navy Yard to deflect mob violence. Prevented from breaching the jail, the mechanics turned their wrath instead on one of the most prosperous African Americans in the city, Beverly Snow, who ran a restaurant, the Epicurean Eating House, then located at the corner of Sixth Street and Pennsylvania Avenue. A free man of mixed race, Snow catered to the city's upper-class white population, serving such delicacies as green turtles and sheep's heads. Snow escaped unharmed into Maryland, but his business was wrecked: the rioters destroyed his furniture, broke his windows, and took or ruined his stock of food and liquor. He later emigrated to Canada.

The mob moved next to the Union Seminary, one of the earliest schools in DC for students of African descent. They destroyed all books, furniture, and tore down part of the building. The mob subsequently burned or destroyed several private homes, a church, another school, and a whorehouse, all owned by African Americans. After a few days, the violence subsided. Bowen was brought to trial, condemned, and given the death sentence.

Bowen was scheduled to hang in February 1836. Thornton, regretting her earlier desire to punish her slave, drew up a petition for a presidential pardon and obtained thirty-four signatures of other prominent white citizens. She wrote a seventeen-page letter to President Andrew Jackson, who responded by postponing Bowen's execution until June. A second appeal by Thornton that summer led to Bowen's full pardon. As part of the settlement, Thornton agreed to sell Bowen to someone outside the city. He was sold for $750. Little more is known of Bowen's subsequent life.

Both of these incidents described in the *Diary* show how precarious Black lives were in DC in the antebellum period. And both show the importance of powerful white allies to intervene legally when slaves' and freemen's lives were endangered.

Shiner died at age seventy-five of smallpox. He was buried in Becketts Cemetery (no longer extant, once located in the block bounded by E and D Streets and Seventeenth and Eighteenth Streets SE, across from Congressional Cemetery).

Anne Lynch Botta

Anne Lynch Botta

November 11, 1815–March 23, 1891

Anne Lynch Botta lived in DC from 1850 to 1853, while serving as personal secretary to Senator Henry Clay. She is the author of *Poems* (1849) and *A Handbook of Universal Literature* (1860, once a widely used textbook), and editor of an anthology, *The Rhode Island Book* (1841).

Born in 1815, Botta was educated at the Albany Female Academy, taught briefly in Albany and Providence, Rhode Island, and, after her sojourn in DC, settled in New York, teaching at the Brooklyn Girls'

Academy, writing freelance articles for magazines, and hosting a renowned salon in her home, frequented by some of the most famous writers of the time, including William Cullen Bryant, Edgar Allen Poe, Helen Hunt Jackson, Margaret Fuller, Ralph Waldo Emerson, Horace Greeley, and Fanny Kemble.

In middle age, she married a Dante Alighieri scholar who taught at New York University. After her death in 1891, her husband compiled her unpublished poems, along with letters and tributes, and published the posthumous *Memoirs of Anne C. L. Botta: Written by Her Friends* (1893).

TO AN ASTRONOMER

Upon the Professor we'll waste not a glance,
    Since he has no eyes for us poor terrestrials;
With his heart can we have any possible chance,
    When he gives us for rivals a host of celestials?
What cares he for eyes, whether hazel or blue,
    Or for any slight charms such as we share between us,—
When, his glass in his hand, he can sit the night through,
    And ogle at leisure Diana and Venus.

WEBSTER

"When I and all those that hear me shall have gone to our last home, and when the mould may have gathered on our memories, as it will on our tombs . . ."
            —Daniel Webster's Speech in the Senate, July, 1850

The mould upon thy memory!—No,
Not while one note is rung,
Of those divine, immortal songs
Milton and Shakespeare sung;—
Not till the night of years enshrouds
The Anglo-Saxon tongue.

No! let the flood of Time roll on,
And men and empires die;—
Genius enthroned on lofty heights
Can its dread course defy,
And here on earth, can claim the gift
Of immortality:

Can save from that Lethean tide
That sweeps so dark along,
A people's name;—a people's fame
To future time prolong,
As Troy still lives and only lives
In Homer's deathless song.

What though to buried Nineveh
The traveller may come,
And roll away the stone that hides
That long forgotten tomb;—
He questions its mute past in vain,
Its oracles are dumb.

What though he stand where Balbec stood
Gigantic in its pride;
No voice comes o'er that silent waste,
Lone, desolate and wide;—
They had no bard, no orator,
No statesman,—and they died.

They lived their little span of life,
They lived and died in vain;—
They sank ingloriously beneath
Oblivion's silent reign,
As sank beneath the Dead Sea wave
The Cities of the Plain.

But for those famed, immortal lands,
Greece and imperial Rome,

Where Genius left its shining mark,
And found its chosen home,
All eloquent with mind they speak,
Wood, wave and crumbling dome.

The honeyed words of Plato still
Float on the echoing air,
The thunders of Demosthenes
Aegean waters bear,
And the pilgrim to the Forum hears
The voice of Tully there.

And thus thy memory shall live,
And thus thy fame resound,
While far-off future ages roll
Their solemn cycles round,
And make this wide, this fair New World
An ancient, classic ground.

Then with our Country's glorious name
Thine own shall be entwined;
Within the Senate's pillared hall
Thine image shall be shrined;
And on the nation's Law shall gleam
Light from thy giant mind.

Our proudest monuments no more
May rise to meet the sky,
The stately Capitol o'erthrown,
Low in the dust may lie;
But mind, sublime above the wreck,
Immortal—cannot die.

The Civil War Era, 1861–1865

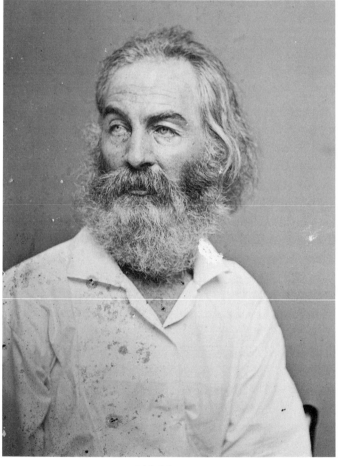

Walt Whitman

Walt Whitman's Downtown

This walking tour focuses on DC's most acclaimed writer of the Civil War period and the years immediately after the war, Walt Whitman. Since the downtown neighborhoods of the city have changed dramatically since Whitman's time, it takes some exercise of the imagination to transport us back to that era.

Whitman traveled from his native Brooklyn to DC in December 1862. He came to find out what happened to his brother George, a Union soldier; a Brooklyn newspaper listed his name among the wounded in the Battle of Fredericksburg but did not elaborate on his wounds. After discovering that George had been grazed by a bullet but had healed, Whitman extended his stay and began to visit the city's many hospitals. At first he sought out other wounded soldiers from Brooklyn but soon gave solace to any who needed care.

Whitman was able to find work as a clerk with the federal government. He wrote occasional pieces for New York and DC newspapers, but his principal vocation was his poetry. During this period, Whitman wrote nearly one hundred new poems, including the war poems of *Drum-Taps* (1865), "Passage to India," and his poems about Abraham Lincoln, "O Captain, My Captain" and "When Lilacs Last in the Dooryard Bloom'd."

Whitman remained in DC from age forty-three to fifty-four. He suffered a stroke in early 1873 and went

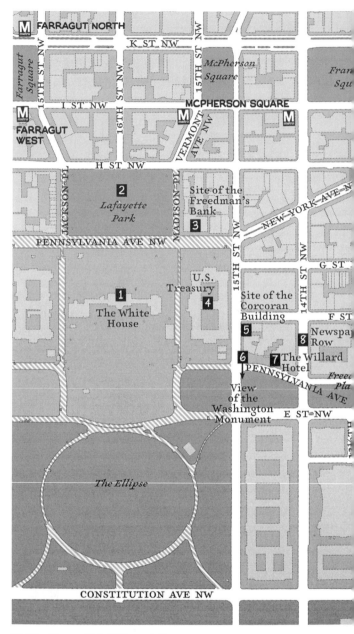

Walking Tour 1: Walt Whitman's Downtown

to stay with the same brother who had brought him to Washington. George was then living in Camden, New Jersey. Whitman never fully recovered, living there as a "half-Paralytic" and continuing to write poetry until his death in 1892.

→ **Take the Metro to MacPherson Square and walk south on Vermont Avenue to Lafayette Park.**

1 The White House

1600 Pennsylvania Avenue NW

Whitman wrote in *Specimen Days* (1882), "I wander about a good deal, sometimes at night under the moon. To-night took a long look at the President's House. The white portico—the palace-like, tall, round columns, spotless as snow—the walls also—the tender and soft moonlight, flooding the pale marble, and making peculiar faint languishing shades, not shadows—everywhere a soft transparent hazy, thin, blue moon-lace, hanging in the air—the brilliant and extra-plentiful clusters of gas, on and around the facade, columns, portico, &c.—everything so white, so marbly pure and dazzling, yet soft—the White House of future poems, and of dreams and dramas, there in the soft and copious moon—the gorgeous front, in the trees, under the lustrous flooding moon, full of reality, full of illusion—the forms of the trees, leafless, silent, in trunk and myriad-angles of branches, under the stars and sky—the White House of the land, and of beauty and night—sentries at the gates, and by the portico, silent, pacing there in blue overcoats—stopping you not at all, but eyeing you with sharp eyes, whichever way you move."

Lafayette Park

Whitman famously loved Lincoln. He wrote: "I think well of the President. He has a face like a hoosier Michael Angelo, so awful ugly it becomes beautiful, with its strange mouth, its deep cut, criss-cross lines, and its doughnut complexion. . . . I more and more rely upon his idiomatic western genius, careless of court dress or court decorums."

2 Lafayette Park

This famous seven-acre park has been used as a slave market, a racetrack, a graveyard, a zoo (established by President Ulysses S. Grant), and the site of innumerable political protests.

In Whitman's time, it would have held only one sculpture, of Andrew Jackson. It would also have held tents, used by the soldiers who guarded the White House. Prominent residents living in the area complained that the soldiers had trampled all the flowers and were hanging their laundry on the statue to dry.

The Jackson statue commemorates the hero of the War of 1812 and was created by Clark Mills. President Millard Fillmore presided over the dedication ceremony in 1853. It was the first equestrian statue in the United States, and Mills, who was self-taught, had never previously worked in bronze.

Decatur House and the Dolley Madison House, on either side of the north end of the park, had been taken over by the federal government during the war, for use as military offices. St. John's Episcopal Church, built in 1816, was standing, and Lincoln attended services there the very first Sunday after he arrived in Washington. (Although he would regularly attend the New York Avenue Presbyterian Church while president, he did sometimes attend services at St. John's, where they still reserve Pew 54 as the "President's Pew.") The Parish House next door was used during the Civil War as the home of the British legation.

A later resident of 23 Madison Place (now razed, and the site of the Howard T. Markey National Courts building) was Robert Ingersoll. Ingersoll was a lawyer whose speeches on atheism, Reconstruction, and women's suffrage made him one of the greatest American orators of the nineteenth century. He committed all his speeches to memory, and some were more than three hours in length. Whitman became friends with Ingersoll, who delivered Whitman's eulogy at his funeral.

No other event of this period would affect Whitman so deeply as the assassination of Abraham Lincoln. He not only wrote poems about Lincoln but also gave annual lectures on the anniversary of the president's death. While Whitman lived in DC, the Rodgers House stood at 17 Madison Place, and was leased to William

Seward, Lincoln's secretary of state. This was the site of Lewis Paine's assassination attempt on April 14, 1865. The plan was for John Wilkes Booth to kill Lincoln and Grant at Ford's Theater, and for George Atzerodt to kill Vice President Andrew Johnson. Atzerodt pulled out at the last minute, and the Grants decided not to go to the theater that night. Paine managed to push his way into Rodgers House, claiming to be a messenger with a prescription from Seward's doctor. Seward was in bed, recovering from a carriage accident, with a broken arm and fractured jaw. Paine injured Seward's two sons and stabbed Seward in the throat and face. Seward healed and resumed his duties as secretary of state. His wife, however, never recovered from the shock, dying two months after the attack.

One of the few original houses preserved along the opposite side of the park is 712 Jackson Place NW, built in the early 1850s, which is also connected to the Lincoln assassination. Near the end of the Civil War, this house was rented by Major Henry Reed Rathbone. When Grant declined to accompany Lincoln to Ford's Theater, he took Rathbone and his fiancée, Clara Harris, instead. Booth stabbed Rathbone's arm during his attack on Lincoln. Rathbone recovered but was left with a lifelong regret that he had been unable to keep Booth from escaping. That is believed to contribute to his final tragedy: in 1894, while on a diplomatic mission in Germany, he killed Clara (then his wife) and tried, unsuccessfully, to take his own life. He spent the remainder of his life in an insane asylum in Hanover, Germany.

→ **Walk across the park to Pennsylvania Avenue, and turn left. Go to the corner of Pennsylvania and Madison Place NW.**

Freedman's Savings Bank, ca. 1890

3 Site of the Freedman's Savings Bank (now the Treasury Annex)

1509 Pennsylvania Avenue NW

In 1870, the Department of Justice was created, by merging the Offices of the Attorney General and the Solicitor of the Treasury. Whitman was in the earliest class of employees of the newly formed department. Beginning in 1871, Whitman's office was in the upper floors of the Freedman's Savings Bank Building, where the Justice employees were consolidated. By January 1872, his employer having outgrown that building, Whitman was transferred to an office in the Treasury Building proper, in the Office of the Solicitor.

The Freedman's Savings and Trust Company, chartered by Congress in 1865, was operated strictly by and for freed slaves. The building, an elegant French Second Empire–style brownstone with a mansard roof, was the most costly bank building in the city at the time, with interiors of black walnut and marble. Unfortunately, trustees mismanaged funds, and the bank closed in 1874. Frederick Douglass was elected president of the institution in 1874, but even his large personal donations of funds and his pleas to Congress to intervene could not save the bank. In 1899, the building was razed. The current building, the Treasury Annex, was built in 1917.

→ **Continue to Fifteenth Street, turn right, and walk half a block.**

4 U.S. Treasury

1500 Pennsylvania Avenue NW

Whitman worked for the Office of the Attorney General from 1865 until 1873, and in 1872–73 his office was in this building, where he worked as a clerk for the newly established Justice Department. His office was on the first floor, facing south. For some time after the war, Whitman processed pardons for former Rebels, as he described in a letter written at the time:

This is the place where the big southerners now come up to get pardoned–all the rich men & big officers of the Reb army have to get special pardons, before they can buy or sell, or do any thing that will stand law–Sometimes there is a steady stream of them coming in here–old & young, men & women–I talk with them often, & find it very interesting to listen to their descriptions of things that have happened down south, & to how things are there now.

Whitman spent some of his off-hours at the Treasury as well, which was better heated and better lit than his boardinghouse rooms. As he noted in a letter to his mother, "I spend quite a good deal of time, evenings & Sundays, in the office at my desk, as I can get into the Treasury building any time, as the door-keepers all know me—nearly all of them are broken down or one-legged soldiers—The office is warm & nice, with gas, & all the modern improvements."

While getting ready to leave on the evening of Sunday, January 23, 1873, Whitman suffered a debilitating stroke.

→ **Look across the street.**

5 Site of the Corcoran Building (now the W Hotel)

515 Fifteenth Street NW

This was the site of the Corcoran Building, where Whitman had his first federal employment, working as a copyist for the U.S. Army paymaster. Whitman's office was on the fifth floor with "a splendid view" of the Potomac River and Georgetown. No provision was made for disabled soldiers; those who wanted to collect their pay before being furloughed had to climb the stairs. Whitman remembered hearing the "clank of crutches" coming toward his office.

Whitman also recalled seeing troops from his window. He wrote about "A long string of army wagons defiling along 15th street, and around into Pennsylvania avenue—white canvas coverings arch them over, and each one has its six-mule team . . . and once or twice a party of cavalry in their yellow-trimmed jacks gallop along."

Next door to the Corcoran Building site is the site of Whitman's last DC residence. Whitman lived in eight boardinghouses while in DC, none of which still stand. Whitman rented an attic room here across the street from the Treasury Building. After his stroke late in the evening on January 23, somehow he managed to drag himself down the office stairs and the few hundred feet to his boardinghouse, then up the stairs to his bed, but that night he awoke and realized he couldn't move his legs. A doctor was called the next morning, and although Whitman did rally somewhat, he was never really well again. His left side was partially paralyzed, and his physician, Dr. William Drinkard, prescribed bed rest and electric shock treatments administered to his legs. At first Peter Doyle and his old friend (and former Boston publisher) Charles Eldridge took turns staying with Whitman during the days and nights, "helping & lifting & nursing me" as he reported to his mother, but as a full recovery began to seem more and more remote, Whitman realized that he would have to make other plans. He was frustrated "to be disabled, so feeble, cannot walk nor do anything, when one's mind & will are just as clear as ever."

6 View of the Washington Monument

In Whitman's day, the Washington Monument, begun in 1848, was only one-third built, a marble stump of 154 feet that he could see from his office window. The U.S.

Capitol dome was not completed either, and the roads were unpaved. The Monument grounds were used as a feedlot and slaughterhouse for cattle that were used to provision Union soldiers, and the area was notable for its noxious smell.

As Philip Callow writes in *From Noon to Starry Night: A Life of Walt Whitman* (1992), DC was

a half-finished city, in confusion now with its trains of army wagons, a hundred or more to a convoy. The rutted roads turned to mud in the first heavy downpour. Pigs rooted in the dirt side streets. Sewage marshes made the air foul around the White House . . . a large population of rootless freed slaves lived wretchedly in shantytowns alongside white colonial mansions. It was a "beginning" place, Whitman was to tell Horace Traubel. "Go into the markets; it's there you find the busiest, most curious native life of the place. Washington has the insane political element—and then it has itself, its resident blacks and whites. You are just on the edge of the South there—you begin to penetrate Dixie."

Callow calls it a place "swamped by a tide of newcomers, office seekers, profiteers, and swindlers, prostitutes, bereaved wives and families, strangers like him hunting for loved ones. . . . Accommodations were scarce, prices rocketing. Deserters and derelicts roamed the night streets."

➜ **Bear left where Pennsylvania and E Street intersect.**

Willard's Hotel during the Civil War

7 Site of Willard's Hotel (now the Willard InterContinental Hotel)

1401 Pennsylvania Avenue NW

Earlier incarnations of Willard's Hotel (as it was then called) could be found on this site as early as 1847. Whitman visited the hotel on occasion during the Civil War. Before coming to DC, Whitman imagined the scene here following the Union rout at First Bull Run: "Resolution, manliness, seems to have abandoned Washington. . . . Willard's is full of shoulder-straps. . . . Sneak, blow, put on airs there in Willard's sumptuous parlors and barrooms or anywhere—no explanation shall save you. Bull Run is your work."

Two brothers, Joseph and Henry Willard, ran the establishment, a favorite of politicians, entertainers, society figures, and diplomats. In 1861, Julia Ward Howe visited from Boston and wrote new words to the tune of "John Brown's Body" in her Willard's Hotel room. The new song became known as "The Battle Hymn of the Republic."

→ **Walk to the corner, and look north up Fourteenth Street.**

8 Newspaper Row

"Newspaper Row" was located along this block of Fourteenth Street in a series of row houses. During the Civil War, newspapers from across the country sent correspondents to Washington, and Whitman, a journalist himself, was a friend to several of the newsmen. Articles he wrote during his Washington years were published in the *New York Times;* he also contributed a few pieces to two local papers, the *Evening Star* and *Morning Chronicle.* This is now, appropriately, the site of the National Press Club, which was founded in 1867.

Journalists who covered the Civil War and were based in DC included Lawrence A. Gobright (Washington bureau chief for the Associated Press), Benjamin Perley Poore (editor of the *Congressional Directory* and a correspondent for Massachusetts papers), William Swinton (correspondent for the *New York Times,* whom Whitman knew previously from his favorite New York hangout, Pfaff's Saloon), Thomas Bailey Aldrich (of the *New York Illustrated News,* also a friend of Whitman's), Hiram J. Ramsdell, Jerome B. Stillson, and George Alfred Townsend (who wrote for several newspapers under the pen name Gath).

Mark Twain was another young journalist who was living in DC (in 1867), but he was then a complete unknown. He finished the manuscript of his book *The Innocents Abroad* (1869) and lived in a boardinghouse popular with journalists that was run by Virginia Wells, conveniently located to Newspaper Row on the northwest corner of Fourteenth and F Streets.

➜ **Enter the plaza on Pennsylvania Avenue between Thirteenth and Fourteenth Streets NW.**

9 Freedom Plaza

Freedom Plaza combines the map Pierre L'Enfant designed for Washington with quotes about the city, etched in the paving stones. Whitman is given two quotes. Look in the southeast corner for: "I went to Washington as everybody goes there prepared to see everything done with some furtive intention, but I was disappointed—pleasantly disappointed." In the northwest corner, you can find: "All known reverence I sum up in you, whoever you are! The President is there in the White House for you—it is not you who are here for the President!"

Somewhere near this spot, Whitman watched the Grand Review of the Union army. The close of the Civil War was celebrated by a parade of troops. As Whitman wrote, "For two days now the broad spaces of Pennsylvania Avenue along to Treasury Hill, and so by detour around to the President's House, and so up to Georgetown, and across the Aqueduct bridge, have been alive with a magnificent sight, the returning armies. In their wide ranks stretching clear across the Avenue, I watch them march or ride along, at a brisk pace, through two whole days—infantry, cavalry, artillery—some 200,000 men."

The National Theater across the street is DC's oldest theater (and one of the oldest theaters in the country); this is the sixth building to occupy this site since 1835. During the Civil War, it was known as Grover's National Theater. Lincoln often attended plays here, as well as at Ford's Theater.

Ford's Theater

→ **Walk east on E Street two blocks, then turn left on Tenth Street NW.**

10 Ford's Theater

516 Tenth Street NW

Ford's Theater is famous as the site of President Lincoln's assassination. Whitman was out of town in April 1865, but his lover Peter Doyle was present in the theater. He gave Whitman a firsthand account to supplement what Whitman read in the newspapers.

Whitman never actually met Lincoln; his devotion was not based on personal knowledge of the president.

But Whitman missed no opportunity to see Lincoln from afar: he even waited on the street to witness Lincoln's summer commute. During the hot summer months, Lincoln slept at the higher, cooler elevation of the Soldier's Home, and traveled by horseback each morning to work in the White House. Whitman wrote, "I see very plainly Abraham Lincoln's dark brown face, with the deep-cut lines, the eyes, always to me with a deep latent sadness in the expression. We have got so that we exchange bows, and very cordial ones."

→ **Continue north on Tenth Street to the end of the block, then turn right on F Street NW, and walk a block and a half.**

⬛11 U.S. Patent Office Building (now the Smithsonian National Portrait Gallery)

Eighth and F Streets NW

Built as the U.S. Patent Office, this is the third-oldest government building in the city, after the White House and the Capitol. The Patent Office was built as a temple to American ingenuity, displaying patent models and designs, natural history specimens, and "curiosities from around the world." During the Civil War, it served as a temporary hospital, where patients were laid on more than two thousand cots between the tall glass display cases filled with patent models. Whitman frequently visited sick and wounded soldiers here, as did Clara Barton.

Whitman wrote: "Two of the immense apartments are fill'd with high and ponderous glass cases, crowded with models in miniature of every kind of utensil, machine, or invention, it ever enter'd into the mind of

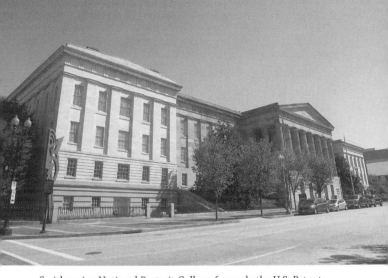

Smithsonian National Portrait Gallery, formerly the U.S. Patent Office Building

man to conceive; and with curiosities and foreign presents. Between these cases are lateral openings, perhaps eight feet wide and quite deep, and in these were placed the sick. . . . Many of them were very bad cases, wounds and amputations." At least fifty-six buildings in Washington were used as war hospitals. Some were specially built for the purpose, but many were existing buildings that were simply requisitioned. Almost every large building was used, even churches.

Whitman wrote in a letter to his mother of the hospital he visited most often: "I devote myself much to Armory Square Hospital because it contains by far the worst cases, most repulsive wounds, has the most suffering & most need of consolation—I go every day without fail, & often at night—sometimes stay very late—no one interferes with me, guards, doctors, nurses, nor any one—I am let to take my own course." That hospital site is today's Smithsonian Air and Space

Museum, located on the south side of the National Mall. It generally got the "worst cases" because it was so near to the docks on the Potomac River where ambulance ships were unloaded.

Whitman recalled that, "Many a soldier's loving arms about this neck have cross'd and rested, / Many a soldier's kiss dwells on these bearded lips."

He seems to have been a natural nurse. His close association with sick and dying soldiers gave him a deeper connection to life and a fuller understanding of human nature. As he wrote in his journal, he had "an instinct & faculty" for easing the suffering of these young wounded men.

Whitman wrote a letter to friends in New York, saying: "These thousands, and tens and twenties of thousands of American young men, badly wounded, all sorts of wounds, operated on, pallid with diarrhea, languishing, dying with fever, pneumonia, &c. open a new world somehow to me, giving closer insights, new things, exploring deeper mines than any yet, showing our humanity. . . . For here I see, not at intervals, but quite always, how certain, man, our American man—how he holds himself cool and unquestioned master above all pains and bloody mutilations. It is immense, the best thing of all, nourishes me of all men." Two months after arriving, he wrote in a letter to his brother Jeff Whitman about why he stayed on in this city: "I cannot give up my hospitals yet. I never before had my feelings so thoroughly and (so far) permanently absorbed, to the very roots, as by these huge swarms of dear, wounded, sick, dying boys—I get very much attached to some of them, and many of them have come to depend on seeing me, and having me sit by them a few minutes, as if for their lives."

A friend reported in an article in the *New York Herald:*

I saw him, time and again, in the Washington hospitals,
or wending his way there with basket or haversack on
his arm, and the strength of beneficence suffusing his
face. His devotion surpassed the devotion of woman. . . .
From cot to cot [soldiers] called him, often in tremulous
tones or in whispers. They embraced him; they touched
his hand; they gazed at him. To one he gave a few words
of cheer; for another he wrote a letter home; to others he
gave an orange, a few comfits, a cigar, a pipe and tobacco,
a sheet of paper or a postage stamp. . . . As he took his
way toward the door, you could hear the voices of many
a stricken hero calling, "Walt, Walt, Walt! Come again!
Come again!"

Roy Morris Jr., in his book *The Better Angel: Walt Whitman in the Civil War* (2001), writes:

"Noxious effluvia"—bad smells—were still believed to
be the chief cause of the rampant infections that raced
unchecked through the hospital wards and carried off
postoperative patients by the thousands. . . . Medical
care in the early 1860s was not much advanced from the
Middle Ages. . . . Typhoid fever, malaria, and diarrhea,
the three most prevalent and deadly killers of the Civil
War, tore through every hospital and camp, spread by
infected drinking water, fecally contaminated food, and
disease-transmitting mosquitoes. Meanwhile, attending
physicians ascribed the ills to "mephitic effluvia," "crowd
poisoning," "sewer emanations," "depressing mental
agencies," "lack of nerve force," "exhalations," "night air,"
"sleeping in damp blankets," "choleric temperament,"
"decay of wood," "odor of horse manure," "effluvia of putre-
fying corpses," and "poisonous fungi in the atmosphere."

The Patent Office Building was also used for Abraham Lincoln's second inaugural ball. Whitman commented on the stark contrast in use: "What a different scene they presented to my view a while since, fill'd with a crowded mass of the worst wounded of the war, brought in from second Bull Run, Antietam, and Fredericksburgh. To-night, beautiful women, perfumes, the violins' sweetness, the polka and the waltz; then, the amputation, the blue face, the groan, the glassy eye of the dying, the clotted rag, the odor of wounds and blood, and many a mother's son amid strangers, passing away untended there."

Whitman worked briefly in this building as well, as a clerk for the Bureau of Indian Affairs. In a letter to his brother Jeff, Whitman wrote: "It is easy enough—I take things very easy—the rule is to come at 9 and go at 4—but I don't come at 9, and only stay till 4 when I want, as at present to finish a letter for the mail—I am treated with great courtesy, as an evidence of which I have to inform you that since I began this letter, I have been sent for by the cashier to receive my PAY for the arduous & invaluable service I have already rendered to the government."

While working for the Bureau of Indian Affairs, Whitman witnessed Cheyenne, Navajo, and Apache chiefs dressed in full ceremonial regalia, who came to see the Indian commissioner about the terms of annuities, supplies, and treaty lands in the West. He wrote a short essay on the experience, which includes a plea for a greater appreciation of the role of the lowly clerk. "In this office," he reported, "most of the business (as an instance of how important one clerk sometimes is,) would probably have to come to a stand-still, or at any rate would be seriously embarrassed, without the presence of Charles E. Mix, the Chief Clerk, who has long been in the Bureau, knows all its parts and antecedents, (has often been Acting Commissioner,) has the executive management of the Bureau and its employees, & is beloved & respected by all of them."

Whitman clearly enjoyed the relaxed atmosphere of this job, but he was fired after only six months, when a new secretary of the interior was named. James Harlan knew of *Leaves of Grass* by reputation only but was incensed to hear that he was employing the author of such an immoral book.

Whitman was able to quickly find a new clerkship after his summary dismissal. In 2011, a noted Whitman scholar, Kenneth M. Price, uncovered a trove of nearly three thousand documents in Whitman's fine handwriting, now in the National Archives, written while he was a clerk for Indian Affairs and in his subsequent job for the Office of the Attorney General.

Long after the end of Civil War—indeed for the rest of his life—Whitman continued to write and publish poetry and prose on the war's impact on American identity. Whitman even claimed that *Leaves of Grass* could not have been written without his wartime experiences (despite the fact that three earlier editions had been published prior to his moving to Washington). For him, the Civil War and how the nation reacted to it were more revealing, and more ennobling, than any other time.

Of the years he spent in DC, Whitman concluded, "I consider [them] the greatest privilege and satisfaction, (with all their feverish excitements and physical deprivations and lamentable sights,) and, of course, the most profound lesson of my life."

Poems by Walt Whitman

WHEN I HEARD AT THE CLOSE OF THE DAY

When I heard at the close of the day how my name had
     been receiv'd with plaudits in the capitol, still it was
     not a happy night for me that follow'd,
And else when I carous'd, or when my plans were
     accomplish'd, still I was not happy,
But the day when I rose at dawn from the bed of perfect
     health, refresh'd, singing, inhaling the ripe breath of
     autumn,
When I saw the full moon in the west grow pale and
     disappear in the morning light,
When I wander'd alone over the beach, and undressing
     bathed, laughing with the cool waters, and saw the
     sun rise,
And when I thought how my dear friend my lover was on
     his way coming, O then I was happy,
O then each breath tasted sweeter, and all that day my
     food nourish'd me more, and the beautiful day pass'd
     well,
And the next came with equal joy, and with the next at
     evening came my friend,
And that night while all was still I heard the waters roll
     slowly continually up the shores,
I heard the hissing rustle of the liquid and sands as
     directed to me whispering to congratulate me,
For the one I love most lay sleeping by me under the same
     cover in the cool night,
In the stillness in the autumn moonbeams his face was
     inclined toward me,
And his arm lay lightly around my breast—and that night
     I was happy.

Vigil strange I kept on the field one night,

When you, my son and my comrade, dropt at my side that
day,

One look I but gave, which your dear eyes return'd, with a
look I shall never forget;

One touch of your hand to mine, O boy, reach'd up as you
lay on the ground;

Then onward I sped in the battle, the even-contested
battle;

Till late in the night reliev'd, to the place at last again I
made my way;

Found you in death so cold, dear comrade—found your
body, son of responding kisses (never again on earth
responding;)

Bared your face in the starlight—curious the scene—cool
blew the moderate night wind;

Long there and then in vigil I stood, dimly around me the
battle-field spreading;

Vigil wondrous and vigil sweet, there in the fragrant silent
night;

But not a tear fell, nor even a long-drawn sigh—Long, long
I gazed;

Then on the earth partially reclining, sat by your side,
leaning my chin in my hands;

Passing sweet hours, immortal and mystic hours with you,
dearest comrade—Not a tear, not a word;

Vigil of silence, love and death—vigil for you, my son and
my soldier,

As onward silently stars aloft, eastward new ones upward
stole;

Vigil final for you, brave boy, (I could not save you, swift
was your death,

I faithfully loved you and cared for you living—I think we
	shall surely meet again;)
Till at latest lingering of the night, indeed just as the dawn
	appear'd,
My comrade I wrapt in his blanket, envelop'd well his
	form,
Folded the blanket well, tucking it carefully over head, and
	carefully under feet;
And there and then, and bathed by the rising sun, my son
	in his grave, in his rude-dug grave I deposited;
Ending my vigil strange with that—vigil of night and
	battle-field dim;
Vigil for boy of responding kisses, (never again on earth
	responding;)
Vigil for comrade swiftly slain—vigil I never forget, how as
	day brighten'd,
I rose from the chill ground, and folded my soldier well in
	his blanket,
And buried him where he fell.

Portraits

John Burroughs

April 3, 1837–March 29, 1921

John Burroughs came to DC during the Civil War to join a work crew that buried Union soldiers. It was horrible work: hard and repugnant labor. He was hoping to make a living as a writer, in particular to develop a literature of nature that combined scientific precision with a sense of awe. But he had, at that time, published very little.

Burroughs had already read and admired Walt Whitman's *Leaves of Grass* when he happened upon him on the street in downtown DC one day in 1864. Burroughs was eighteen years younger than Whitman, and he quickly became a disciple of the older writer. Burroughs wrote:

One thing I plume myself upon in this world, and that is that I saw the greatness of the poet from the first—that no disguise of the common, the near, the rough, the "tramp," could conceal from me the divinity that was back of it all, and challenged me to the contest. Familiar intercourse with him did not blur this impression. That head, that presence, those words of love and wisdom convinced like Nature herself. I pitied those who saw him, and yet saw him not.

Burroughs's other main influences were the Transcendentalists, particularly Ralph Waldo Emerson and

John Burroughs

Henry David Thoreau, and the British Romantic poet William Wordsworth. But Whitman would have the most significant and long-lasting influence on his writing. Burroughs's passion for birds would affect Whitman in turn: he provided the information on the hermit thrush that became a major symbol for Whitman's "When Lilacs Last in the Dooryard Bloom'd" and on the eagles in "A Dalliance of Eagles." Burroughs wrote two books about their friendship. *Notes on Walt Whitman as Poet and Person* (1867) was heavily revised by Whitman and should rightly be considered a collaboration, although it bears Burroughs's name, and *Whitman, A Study* (1896) was written after Whitman's death.

Burroughs would go on to write twenty-seven books of nonfiction, becoming one of the most respected authors of his time. Many of his essays first appeared in popular magazines and were adopted by public school curricula across the United States. He is credited with developing a particularly American form of nature essay and helping to define and develop the U.S. conservation movement.

When he secured a job with the U.S. Treasury, Burroughs was able to begin preparing a first book of nature essays in earnest, with the encouragement of Whitman. Some of that book, *Wake Robin* (1871), is set in and around DC, particularly in Rock Creek Park. Burroughs would later become a federal bank examiner, and he left DC in 1874 to return to his beloved Upstate New York. He is remembered in DC with an elementary school named in his honor.

Here is an excerpt from *Wake Robin,* from the essay "Spring at the Capital with an Eye to the Birds":

One need but pass the boundary of Washington city to be fairly in the country, and ten minutes' walk in the country brings one to real primitive woods. The town has not yet overflowed its limits like the great Northern commercial capitals, and Nature, wild and unkempt, comes up to its very threshold, and even in many places crosses it. . . .

All parks and public grounds about the city are full of blackbirds. They are especially plentiful in the trees about the White House, breeding there and waging war on all other birds. The occupants of one of the offices in the west wing of the Treasury one day had their attention attracted by some object striking violently against one of the window-panes. Looking up, they beheld a crow blackbird pausing in midair, a few feet from the window. On the broad stone window-sill lay the quivering form of a purple finch. The little tragedy was easily read. The blackbird had pursued the finch with such murderous violence that the latter, in its desperate efforts to escape, had sought refuge in the Treasury. The force of the concussion against the heavy plateglass of the window had killed the poor thing instantly. The pursuer, no doubt astonished at the sudden and novel termination of the career of its victim, hovered for a moment, as if to be sure of what had happened, and made off. . . .

The Capitol grounds, with their fine large trees of many varieties, draw many kinds of birds. In the rear of the building the extensive grounds are peculiarly attractive, being a gentle slope, warm and protected, and quite thickly wooded. Here in early spring I go to hear the robins, catbirds, blackbirds, wrens, etc. In March the white-throated and white-crowned sparrows may be seen, hopping about on the flower-beds or peering slyly from the evergreens. The robin hops about freely upon the grass, notwithstanding the keepers' large-lettered warning, and at intervals, and especially at sunset, carols from the treetops his loud, hearty strain. . . .

Outside of the city limits, the great point of interest to the rambler and lover of nature is the Rock Creek region. Rock Creek is a large, rough, rapid stream, which has its source in the interior of Maryland, and flows in to the Potomac between Washington and Georgetown. Its course, for five or six miles out of Washington, is marked by great diversity of scenery. Flowing in a deep valley, which now and then becomes a wild gorge with overhanging rocks and high precipitous headlands, for the most part wooded; here reposing in long, dark reaches, there sweeping and hurrying around a sudden bend or over a rocky bed; receiving at short intervals small runs and spring rivulets, which open up vistas and outlooks to the right and left, of the most charming description,—Rock Creek has an abundance of all the elements that make up not only pleasing but wild and rugged scenery. There is perhaps, not another city in the Union that has on its very threshold so much natural beauty and grandeur, such as men seek for in remote forests and mountains. A few touches of art would convert this whole region, extending from Georgetown to what is known as Crystal Springs, not more than two miles from the present State Department, into a park unequaled by anything in the world. There are passages between these two points as wild and savage, and apparently as remote from civilization, as anything one meets with in the mountain sources of the Hudson or the Delaware.

One of the tributaries to Rock Creek within this limit is called Piney Branch. It is a small, noisy brook, flowing through a valley of great natural beauty and pictur-esqueness, shaded nearly all the way by woods of oak, chestnut, and beech, and abounding in dark recesses and hidden retreats. . . .

It is not till about the first of April that many wild flowers may be looked for. By this time the hepatica, anemone saxifrage, arbutus, houstonia, and bloodroot may be counted on. A week later, the claytonia or spring beauty, water-cress, violets, a low buttercup, vetch, coryd-alis, and potentilla appear. These comprise most of the April flowers, and may be found in great profusion in the Rock Creek and Piney Branch region.

In each little valley or spring run, some one species predominates. I know invariably where to look for the first liverwort, and where the largest and finest may be found. On a dry, gravelly, half-wooded hill-slope the bird's-foot violet grows in great abundance, and is sparse in neighbor-ing districts. This flower, which I never saw in the North, is the most beautiful and showy of all the violets, and calls forth rapturous applause from all persons who visit the woods. It grows in little groups and clusters, and bears a close resemblance to the pansies of the gardens. Its two purple, velvety petals seem to fall over tiny shoulders like a rich cape. . . .

Emerging from these woods toward the city, one sees the white dome of the Capitol soaring over the green swell of earth immediately in front, and lifting its four thousand tons of iron gracefully and lightly into the air. Of all the sights in Washington, that which will survive the longest in my memory is the vision of the great dome thus rising cloud-like above the hills.

Solomon G. Brown

February 13, 1829–June 24, 1906

Here is a fact you cannot hide,
The Blackman is our country's pride;
May twist and turn it as you will—
The Negro is your brother still.

This fact he loves above the rest;
While it disturbs the white man's rest;
Twist and turn it as you may,
The Negro's here, HE'S HERE TO STAY!

—From "He Is a Negro Still"

In his book *Men of Mark: Eminent, Progressive and Rising* (1887), William J. Simmons describes Solomon G. Brown with a long list of attributes: "Distinguished Scientist, Lecturer, Chief Clerk of the Transportation Department of the Smithsonian Institute, Entomologist, Taxidermist, Lecturer on Insects and Geology."

Solomon G. Brown

Born of free parents in Washington, DC, Brown was the fourth son of Isaac and Rachel Brown. Simmons states: "He was deprived of the common school education by the loss of his father in 1833, when his mother was left a widow, and had at that time six children. They were very poor. His father's property was seized for pretended debts in 1834, leaving the family penniless and homeless. Solomon was early placed under the care of a Mr. Lambert Tree, assistant postmaster in the city post-office."

In the chapbook *Kind Regards of S. G. Brown* (1983), released by the Smithsonian Institution, the authors write: "Whether he was apprenticed to learn a trade (a custom of the day) or become a household servant is unknown. But it is clear that an amicable relationship developed between Brown and the man who became his benefactor." Tree got Brown a good job and appeared as a witness in the District of Columbia Court on his behalf, to confirm his status as a free man.

Brown worked in the post office beginning in 1844, when he was fifteen years old, and in 1845 he was detailed to assist in the construction of the first telegraph system from Baltimore to Washington. (Brown later stated that he was the messenger who carried the first telegraph message to the White House.) Subsequently, he worked as a packer for Gillman & Brothers chemical manufacturing until 1852.

"Mr. Brown was a natural scientist," Simmons continues, "and coming in contact with these learned men only increased his thirst for knowledge. He is a man of rare scientific acquirements, very unassuming in his appearance, and yet his intelligence would astonish one on making his acquaintance."

In 1852, at age twenty-three, Brown began work in the Transportation Department of the new Smithsonian Institution. He was subsequently appointed to the foreign exchange division, where he would serve as a highly regarded clerk, and in 1869 he became the institution's first African American registrar. In addition, he provided scientific and educational illustrations for lectures and publications. The first African American employee of the Smithsonian, he worked there for fifty-four years, retiring in 1906 at the age of seventy-seven. He died in his home just a few months later.

According to the Smithsonian archives, Brown "had many positions while at the Smithsonian, including working as a general laborer building exhibit cases and moving and cleaning furniture, assisting in preparing maps and drawings for Smithsonian lectures, and working in the International Exchange Service. Brown was also listed in Smithsonian annual reports with the title, 'Clerk, In charge of Transportation.'" He developed a close relationship with Spencer Baird while Baird served as assistant secretary, and then secretary of the Institution. The Smithsonian has a collection of Brown's letters to Baird, and one wartime letter, written July 15, 1864, is of particular interest:

All here is well—many have been much frightened at the annual visit of the Rebels to their friends at Maryland, but we are told that the Johnny Rebs are returning home with lots of presents . . . we are also told here that among many other funny things they performed that they knocked but the door of Washington was not opened unto them . . . so they marched off much to the joy and comfort of a greatly excited populace of this city . . . when the report came in that the Rebels had left for the South, to see the great number of brave fighting men that came out from their hiding places and paraded through streets in search of arms to meet the Rebels. But they was mustered out to return to their several dens i.e. the drinking saloons, gambling halls and after hour places to fight the enemy themselves, for it was impossible for decently disposed persons to pass certain localities without being interfered with by these brave men who wanted to fight when the Rebels had gone.

He concludes the letter with a postscript about some of the Smithsonian Institution's most valuable papers, which were entrusted to him: "I had prepared a place in center of the coal cellar under south tower under stone floor for the deposition of a box of valuables committed to my care should any thing suddenly turn up to prevent them being shipped to a place of safety outside of town."

Brown worked under three secretaries of the Smithsonian, Joseph Henry, Spencer Baird, and Samuel P. Langley. In 1902, Langley honored Brown in a small ceremony "upon his reaching fifty years continued service in the Institution." Brown, in turn, presented Langley with a poem written specifically for the occasion, "Fifty Years To-Day," noting the accomplishments of each secretary in turn. (The poem also mentions two other eminent men Brown knew well: George Brown Goode, an ichthyologist and the director of the National Museum at the Smithsonian under Baird, and Samuel F. B. Morse, a painter, codeveloper of Morse code, and a contributor to the invention of the single-wire telegraph system.)

In addition to his work for the Smithsonian, Brown was dedicated to public service. Most notably, he was a legislator, elected three consecutive times (1871–74) by white and African American voters from the Anacostia section of the city to the House of Delegates of the Territorial Government of the District of Columbia.

His honorary positions and volunteer service were wide and varied, including:

Trustee, Wilberforce University
Trustee, Fifteenth Street Presbyterian Church
Superintendent, North Washington Mission Sunday
    School

Member, Freedmen's Relief Association
Trustee, DC Public Schools (Colored)
Grand Secretary, District Grand Lodge of Masons
Commissioner for the Poor, County of Washington
Assistant Honorary Commissioner, DC Committee
    (Colored), of the New Orleans Exposition
President, National Union League
Executive Committee, Emancipation Monument
Honorary Member, Galbraith Lyceum
Corresponding Member, St. Paul Lyceum, Baltimore
Director, Industrial Saving and Building Association
Washington Correspondent, *Anglo-African Christian
    Recorder*
Superintendent, Pioneer Sunday School Association
    of Hillsdale
Editor, "Sunday School Circle," *Jackson (TN) Christian
    Index*

Brown was one of the first residents of the Hillsdale section of Anacostia (originally known as Barry's Farm, when that area was settled primarily by freed slaves following the Civil War), and an active member of the Hillsdale Pioneer Association. He was one of a group of citizens who lobbied the Freedmen's Bureau to purchase the 375-acre Barry Farm tract specifically for homesteading by African American families. He purchased two lots on Elvans Road.

According to the DC Historic Preservation Office brochure *Anacostia Historic District* (2006), Barry's Farm was a planned community started in 1867 by the Freedmen's Bureau to encourage home ownership: "Freedmen were hired to do the initial site-development work, clearing land and cutting roads for a daily wage of $1.25. . . . The cleared land was subdivided into one-acre lots which were sold to the individual purchasers together with enough lumber to build a small house. Carpenters were assigned to assist the freedmen with building. The cost was $125 to $300 for each family."

The neighborhood was later renamed Hillsdale after the first public school, Hillsdale School, opened. Most of those original homes were lost to urban renewal projects, including construction of the Suitland Parkway and the development of a low-rise public housing development. Brown's house on Elvans Road no longer stands.

Brown married a woman named Lucinda (maiden name unknown) on June 16, 1864. Although they had no children, they adopted a niece, Kate Adams, and raised her in their home. They also took in boarders, some of whom lived with them over long periods and became part of their extended family, such as the public school teacher William J. Simmons.

Brown began lecturing on scientific topics as early as 1855. His first lecture was delivered on January 10, 1855, to the Young Peoples' Literary Society and Lyceum, Israel A.M.E. Church, DC. Brown created forty-nine diagrams and illustrations to accompany his lecture, which was entitled "The Social Habits of Insects."

He was also called upon regularly to present his poems to a wide variety of African American societies and groups in the region. In a poetry broadside commissioned by and disseminated at the Colored Men's National Convention held in Washington, DC, on February 3, 1890, Brown's poem "Dear Friends, What's Aroused You?" contains the following lines on the failures of Reconstruction:

Most of these brethren are here from the South;
We read of your suff'rings, now we'll hear from your
    mouth;

. . . .

You come not as beggars for bread nor for meat,
Nor did you come begging congressional seat;
Nor for any party, but for one common cause,
And are seeking for justice that's found in the laws.

. . . .

We died on your fields with our brothers in white;
We never forsook them by day nor by night.

. . . .

And now we have come to demand what is due;
We demand such protection that's accorded to you.

. . . .

We demand what is given to every white face;
We deem that our color is not a disgrace.

How can we be silent and see brothers hung?
From the hands of black voters the ballot is wrung.
See natives shot down for expressing their choice;
Then count out his ballot, deny him his voice.

. . . .

We know of no country, but the land of our birth;
We love and revere it more than any on earth;
If our early ancestors did come from abroad,
Still this is our country, your God is our Lord.

. . . .

A black is selected and marked out to die;
And then he is haltered, he knows not for why;
There has been no indictment; he's swung to a tree;
And this is as frequent as frequent can be.

. . . .

The chief of this nation: why don't he arise.
Arrest these masked demons who the country defies?

God's vengeance is creeping! the time's near at hand;
His justice, long sleeping, will burst o'er the land!
Such fearful outrages against the black race
Will curse this fair nation with darkest disgrace!

According to *Lincoln's Other White House: The Untold Story of the Man and His Presidency* (2005), by Elizabeth Smith Brownstein, Brown was "a kind of Renaissance man who was also a published poet, lecturer on geology to black audiences, organizer of black history tours, and contributor of specimens of local flora and fauna to the Smithsonian's growing collections."

The *Christian Recorder,* on December 27, 1862, called him "really the colored *philosopher* of the United States."

The *Washington Bee,* on July 13 1901, noting that Brown was formerly the "poet laureate of the Philomathian Literary Society," described him as "the best informed Negro in the United States." The *Bee* also called him "the Longfellow of the Negro Race."

Here is an excerpt of his poem "Time Dealing with Man," which was printed in the *Washington Bee* on January 15, 1887:

TIME DEALING WITH MAN

Awake, arise, stand up as men, none can do your part,
Nothing is accomplished here, except you make the start,
Begin just at the starting place, end when you are done,
Time will pay what wages due, at your setting sun.

Charlotte Forten Grimké

August 17, 1837–July 23, 1914

Charlotte Forten Grimké was born into the leading free African American family of Philadelphia. She was an ardent abolitionist and taught freed slaves on St. Helena Island, South Carolina, for two years at the end of the Civil War. After that time, she settled in Washington, DC, where she worked in an administrative position at the Sumner High School, and for the U.S. Treasury Department (where she was one of fifteen hired out of a field of almost five hundred candidates). She gave up this work upon her marriage to the Reverend Francis James Grimké in 1878, at age forty-one. Their only child, a daughter named Theodora, died in infancy.

Grimké's health was frail throughout her life; she had a recurrent problem as a child with a condition described as "lung fever" and also experienced periods of depression. Her husband was thirteen years her junior; his sermons had gained national repute for their vigorous defense of African Americans. Her best-known works during her lifetime were her articles published in mainstream white magazines: "Life on the Sea Islands" (published in the *Atlantic Monthly,* 1864) and "Personal Recollections of Whittier" (published in *New England Magazine,* 1893).

Between 1855 and the late 1890s, Grimké published fifteen poems in such journals as the *Liberator* and *Anglo American,* and approximately the same number of essays in the *Atlantic Monthly* and African American periodicals. She also kept a diary that was published posthumously in 1953.

Grimké was active in the Fifteenth Street Presbyterian Church, where her husband was minister. She

Charlotte Forten Grimké

was also a cofounder and one of the most active members of the Colored Women's League, organized in 1892 and a forerunner of the National Association of Colored Women.

Beginning in 1887, she also opened her home for a weekly Sunday-evening salon where participants could discuss literature, visual arts, music, and other subjects of intellectual interest, as well as issues of civil rights. Meeting on Friday evenings from eight to ten o'clock, the group became known as the Art Club. Grimké's salons and parties made her home a social and cultural center. Her house at 1608 R Street NW in DC is listed on the National Register of Historic Places and marked with a historic plaque.

She later helped organize the Booklovers, a private club that was initially limited to a dozen African American women of the highest social standing. According to *Aristocrats of Color: The Black Elite, 1880–1920* (2000) by Willard B. Gatewood: "Interspersed among programs devoted to Shakespeare and Wagner and to reports on members' European travel, were some that dealt with 'child-rearing practices,' heredity, and similar family-related topics. Not until 1939 did the Booklovers expand their membership and then only by one member, from twelve to thirteen."

Grimké's mixed-race family was impressive for its activism and literary ambitions. In addition to her husband, who wrote sermons, essays, and poetry, served on the Board of Howard University, and helped to establish the American Negro Academy, her family included brother-in-law Archibald H. Grimké, an author, lecturer, and attorney; grandfather James Forten, a famous abolitionist; and a niece who lived with her for part of her youth, the poet and educator Angelina Weld Grimké.

At the end of the Civil War, Grimké witnessed the Grand Review, the military parade of the victorious Union army that took place along Pennsylvania Avenue on May 23 and May 24, 1865. Soldiers from the Army of the Tennessee, the Army of Georgia, and the Army of the Potomac marched from Capitol Hill to the reviewing stand in front of the White House, where they were met by President Andrew Johnson, General-in-Chief Ulysses S. Grant, and leaders from the military and the government. The parade took six hours on two successive days.

Grimké wrote the following tribute:

THE GATHERING OF THE GRAND ARMY

Through all the city's streets there poured a flood,
A flood of human souls, eager, intent;
One thought, one purpose stirred the people's blood,
And through their veins its quickening current sent.

The flags waved gayly in the summer air,
O'er patient watchers 'neath the clouded skies;
Old age, and youth, and infancy were there,
The glad light shining in expectant eyes.

And when at last our country's saviors came,—
In proud procession down the crowded street,
Still brighter burned the patriotic flame,
And loud acclaims leaped forth their steps to greet.

And now the veterans scarred and maimed appear,
And now the tattered battle-flags uprise;
A silence deep one moment fills the air,
Then shout on shout ascends unto the skies.

Oh, brothers, ye have borne the battle strain,
And ye have felt it through the ling'ring years;
For all your valiant deeds, your hours of pain,
We can but give to you our grateful tears!

And now, with heads bowed low, and tear-filled eyes
We see a Silent Army passing slow;
For it no music swells, no shouts arise,
But silent blessings from our full hearts flow.

The dead, the living,—All,—a glorious host,
A "cloud of witnesses,"—around us press—
Shall we, like them, stand faithful at our post,
Or weakly yield, unequal to the stress?

Shall it be said the land they fought to save,
Ungrateful now, proves faithless to her trust?

Shall it be said the sons of sires so brave
Now trail her scarred banner in the dust?

Ah, no! again shall rise the people's voice
As once it rose in accents clear and high—
"Oh, outraged brother, lift your head, rejoice!
Justice shall reign,—Insult and Wrong shall die!"

So shall this day the joyous promise be
Of golden days for our fair land in store;
When Freedom's flag shall float above the free,
And Love and Peace prevail from shore to shore.

Reconstruction, 1865–1878

Paul Laurence Dunbar

Alice Dunbar-Nelson

Paul Laurence Dunbar and Alice Dunbar-Nelson in LeDroit Park

This tour focuses on two remarkable writers, Paul Laurence Dunbar and his wife, Alice Moore Dunbar-Nelson. It also provides context for their lives in DC, discussing the African American intelligentsia who were drawn to LeDroit Park and the surrounding Shaw neighborhood in the years between the end of the Civil War and the beginning of World War II.

Paul Laurence Dunbar was the first African American poet to become nationally known. Although he lived only to the age of thirty-three, he published seventeen books in his lifetime. His books of poems include *Oak and Ivy* (1892), *Majors and Minors* (1895), *Lyrics of a Lowly Life* (1896), *Poems of Cabin and Field* (1899), *When Malindy Sings* (1903), and *Lyrics of Sunshine and Shadow* (1905). His novels and books of short fiction include *The Uncalled* (1898), *Folks from Dixie* (1898), *The Strength of Gideon* (1900), and *The Sport of the Gods* (1902). He also wrote the lyrics for *In Dahomey,* the first musical written and performed entirely by African Americans to appear on Broadway.

Alice Moore Dunbar-Nelson wrote poetry, fiction, and journalism; taught high school; and was an activist for civil rights and women's rights. Her two books are *Violets and Other Tales* (1895) and *The Goodness of St.*

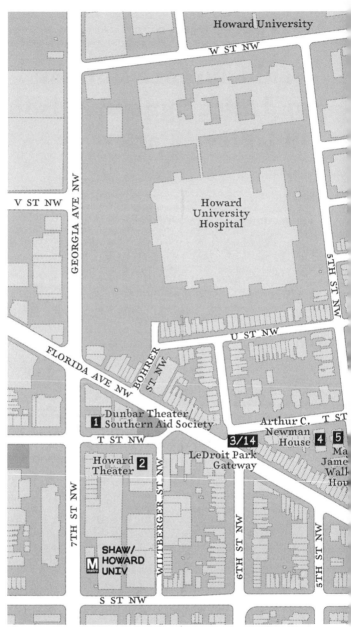

Walking Tour 2: Paul Laurence Dunbar and Alice Dunbar-Nelson in LeDroit Park

Rocque (1899). She also edited *Masterpieces of Negro Elo-quence* (1914) and *The Dunbar Speaker and Entertainer* (1920). She was a regular columnist for the *Pittsburgh Courier* and the *Washington Eagle* and coeditor of the *A.M.E. Review*. In addition, she served as a Mid-Atlantic field organizer for women's suffrage, was a represen-tative for the Woman's Committee on the Council of Defense, and was a popular speaker to a wide range of groups. Her diary, *Give Us Each Day: The Diary of Alice Dunbar-Nelson* (1984), edited by Gloria T. Hull, was published posthumously.

The two married in 1898 and moved to DC, where Dunbar briefly took a job at the Library of Congress. In 1900, diagnosed with tuberculosis and alcoholic, he left the area to try to regain his health. He returned to DC briefly, but the pair separated in 1902 (but never divorced), and Dunbar returned to his mother's home in Dayton, Ohio, where he died in 1906. Dunbar-Nelson remained in the area, living in Maryland and Delaware but returning often to DC, where she was an active member of Georgia Douglas Johnson's literary salon. She married two more times, but always retained her eminent first husband's last name.

➔ **Start at the Shaw-Howard Metro Station (northbound exit). Walk one block north on Seventh Street to the corner of T Street NW.**

1 Dunbar Theater/Southern Aid Society Building

1901 Seventh Street NW

Three prominent institutions in DC were named for Paul Laurence Dunbar. The most important of these

Dunbar Theater

was Dunbar High School, which originally opened as M Street High School but needed to be renamed when the school relocated to New Jersey Avenue. Dunbar High was the most prestigious public school for African American students in the country prior to desegregation. In 1918, twelve years after Paul's death, a play of Alice's, *Mine Eyes Have Seen,* had its premiere at Dunbar High.

In addition, Dunbar Hotel opened in 1946 at the corner of Fifteenth and U Streets. It was the city's most elegant African American hotel for a couple of decades. Originally built as the Portner Flats Apartments in 1902, the building was razed in 1974.

The movie theater named for Dunbar opened in this building in 1920. It was on the ground floor of the Southern Aid Society Building, which also included a pool hall in the basement, several office spaces on the upper floors, as well as the headquarters of the Southern Aid Society, the oldest life insurance company for African Americans in the United States. The building was designed by the prominent black architect Isaiah Hatton just after the end of World War I, as the African American middle class in DC was rapidly expanding.

According to *Leading the Race: The Transformation of the Black Elite in the Nation's Capital, 1880–1920* (1999) by Jacqueline M. Moore:

As a border city, Washington held greater opportunities for economic advancement for African Americans throughout the Progressive Era than any other city in the South. The government provided clerkships, the school system and Howard University offered teaching positions, and the press required editors and printers, not to mention the fact that the size of the black community was large enough to support a limited professional class. The boom in the building trades to accommodate the influx of people during the Civil War provided opportunities for black contractors and architects.

→ **Turn right on T Street and walk one block.**

2 Howard Theater

620 T Street NW

This was the nation's first full-sized theater built for African American patrons, and it was a premier showcase for such performers as Duke Ellington, Ella Fitzgerald, "Moms" Mabley, Pearl Bailey, Sarah Vaughn, and Lena Horne. When it opened in August 1910, DC African American society came out in force to support the venue. The popular "Amateur Nights" at the

Howard Theater

Howard started two decades before the Apollo Theater in New York adopted them.

The theater closed in 1929, a casualty of the Great Depression, but reopened in 1931 and remained popular through the neighborhood's slow decline, closing again in 1970, two years after the riots that decimated parts of Shaw following the assassination of Martin Luther King Jr. The theater was added to the National Register of Historic Places in 1974, but renovations did not begin until 2010. The Howard began a new era when it reopened in April 2012.

Although it was built after Paul Laurence Dunbar's death, Alice would have been familiar with this establishment and may well have attended concerts or other events here in the 1920s.

→ **Continue past the theater and cross Florida Avenue, picking up T Street again on the other side, where**

Florida, T, and Sixth Streets intersect. This is the entrance to the LeDroit Park neighborhood, marked with a metal gateway.

3 LeDroit Park

A planned suburb of less than one square mile, LeDroit Park was developed by Amzi L. Barber, a white professor at Howard University. Although founded to educate African Americans, Howard has always had a multicultural faculty (and the administration was initially all white). The original residents of LeDroit Park were white, and most of the original residents, like Barber, taught or were administrators at Howard.

Between 1873 and 1877, sixty-four picturesque houses were designed by the architect James H. McGill in the eclectic Victorian styles popular at the time: Gothic Revival, Italianate, Second Empire, and Queen Anne. About thirty of those original houses still stand. Streets were originally named for trees, and a fence surrounded the neighborhood. In July 1888, an angry mob of African Americans, mostly Howard University students, tore the fence down, an act that was repeated each time it was rebuilt, until a series of lawsuits were settled and what newspapers at the time termed "the most famous fence in the country" was torn down for good in 1901.

The neighborhood is notable for its proximity not only to Howard but also to Griffith Stadium, the baseball park that stood from 1911 to 1965 (on land where Howard University Hospital now stands). Griffith Stadium was the home to both the segregated baseball teams from DC and was one of the few unsegregated places of entertainment in the city during Reconstruction and after.

The switch from a white to an African American neighborhood took place extremely quickly. Once black families began moving in, it was only a decade before the turnover was complete. By World War I, LeDroit Park had become one of the most desirable African American neighborhoods in the city. Dunbar wrote that it was the place where "comes together the flower of colored citizenship from all parts of the country."

4 Arthur C. Newman House

504 T Street NW

Newman taught in the DC Public Schools, rising to become principal of Armstrong Technical High School and leaving that job to enlist in the U.S. Army. Captain Newman served in World War I and later commanded the local National Guard unit, the First Separate Battalion of DC. He married the sister of Major James E. Walker and settled in next door to his eminent brother-in-law.

5 Major James E. Walker House

502 T Street NW

For twenty-four years, Major Walker served as a teacher, principal, and administrator in the DC Public Schools. He moved to this address in 1909 with his wife, Beatrice. The son of a slave, Walker served with the First Separate Battalion of the U.S. Army, which policed the Mexican border in 1916 and then became the first unit activated to defend the capital prior to U.S. entry into World War I. Because he contracted tuberculosis, Walker did not join his unit for combat in

Europe. When he died in 1918, he was buried in Arlington National Cemetery.

Walker's son, James Walker Jr., inherited the house and opened his dental practice here in later years. The remains of his original sign can be seen on the wall by the entrance, preserved by the new owners.

Both Major Walker and his brother-in-law pursued two of the few more prestigious professions open to African Americans in DC at that time: teacher and soldier. Any jobs at Howard University or in the segregated DC public schools were well respected and well paid. Other good jobs included the ministry, medical professions, journalism, and government clerkships.

But according to *Aristocrats of Color: The Black Elite, 1880–1920* (2000), by Willard B. Gatewood:

Beginning in the 1890s, as the economic depression drew a new wave of black migrants into Washington. . . . [A]n increasingly virulent racism resulted in the decline in federal employment of blacks [which] seriously eroded the fragile economic basis on which the colored aristocracy rested. The number of black federal employees in Washington shrank from 1,532 in 1892 to 1,450 in 1908. Of these latter only about 300 were clerks; the rest were messengers and common laborers. Promotions became increasingly rare. . . . Negro congressmen had usually occupied prominent places in Washington's colored society and provided blacks with access to the federal establishments, but the departure of George H. White of North Carolina in 1901 left Congress without a black member for almost a generation . . . white-collar employment opportunities for blacks outside the government steadily declined. . . . The city's only black bank, the Capital Savings Bank, in which John R. Lynch and Robert Terrell were officers, failed in 1903.

Terrell was another neighbor; we will pass his house later in the tour. Gatewood continues:

Increasingly, restaurants, hotels, theatres, and other public places became inaccessible to upper-class blacks . . . opportunities for white-collar employment shrank so dramatically that blacks, no matter how well educated or refined, were left with only a few menial occupations open to them. "We can't all be preachers, teachers, doctors and lawyers," one upper-class black resident of Washington despaired. . . . Changes in the system in 1901 resulted in the reduction of the office of Superintendent of the Colored Schools to an assistant superintendency. More important in some respects was the replacing of blacks with whites as directors of departments in the Negro school system.

→ **Cross Fifth Street and continue east on T. As you cross the street, be sure to notice the handsome clock tower on the Founder's Library of Howard University, a reminder of how the university's proximity dominated the neighborhood's growth.**

⑥ Dr. Ernest E. and Ethel Highwarden Just House

412 T Street NW

Dr. Just was one of LeDroit Park's most distinguished residents, a longtime Howard professor, and a world-renowned scientist who trained in marine biology at the National Laboratory in Woods Hole, Massachusetts, and whose experiments in embryology, fertilization, and cellular physiology won him a Spingarn Medal in 1915. In addition to teaching at Howard

Medical School, he founded the Department of Zoology, cofounded Omega Psi Phi (the first fraternity founded at a traditionally black college), and cofounded the first campus Dramatic Club. He wrote two books: *Basic Methods for Experiments on Eggs of Marine Animals* (1922) and *The Biology of the Cell Surface* (1939).

His wife, Ethel, was a college graduate in an era when few women of any race pursued higher education. The Justs raised two children, Highwarden and Maribel, in this house, remaining here through the late 1930s. The couple separated when Ernest moved to Europe to pursue his research under less racist conditions; while in Germany, he met the woman who would become his second wife. He returned to the United States in 1941 with his new wife (and a newborn child) but died of cancer soon after.

→ **Turn left on Fourth Street and walk two blocks.**

7 Dunbar House

1934 Fourth Street NW

Paul began corresponding with Alice in 1895, after reading a poem of hers in a Boston magazine. Over the course of two years, the correspondence grew increasingly more intimate. According to *Color, Sex and Poetry: Three Women Writers of the Harlem Renaissance* (1987) by Gloria T. Hull: "When they finally met in New York City on the eve of his February 6, 1897, departure for a reading tour of England, they became engaged. Her work in Brooklyn and his in the Library of Congress, Washington, DC, kept them separated" for five months, but "they finally made their initially secret marriage public, and Alice joined him in Washington,

Dunbar House in LeDroit Park

where they became a glittering part of the city's black society." They were together for only four years in DC, from 1898 to 1902.

Their marriage was not a happy one: "Three months after they began living together, they had a serious enough quarrel that Alice left Washington to stay for a time in West Medford. She insisted that she loved and missed Paul terribly but could not take his moodiness and temper." Paul's mother, Matilda, shared their DC home, which may also have created additional tension.

There is evidence of physical abuse: "More concrete problems arose from their frequent separations because of Paul's engagements, his alcoholism (mistakenly induced by a doctor who prescribed liquor to alleviate his tuberculosis symptoms), and his dependency on heroin tablets."

This house was rented from Robert R. Church, father of Mary Church Terrell, who at that time lived next door. Mary Church Terrell wrote:

Mr. Dunbar was a man of charming personality, with a bold, warm, buoyant humor of character which manifested itself delightfully to his friends. Mingled with his affability of manner were a dignity and poise of bearing which prevented the overbold from coming too near. While there was nothing intrusive or forward about Paul Dunbar, when he found himself among eminent scholars or distinguished people in the highest social circles, he showed both by his manner and his conversation that he felt he was just exactly where he was entitled to be. There was nothing that smacked of truckling, and nobody in the wildest flight of imagination could dream that Paul Dunbar felt particularly flattered at the attention he received. The maturity of the intellectual power was manifested in his conversation as well as in his writing, and his fund of information was remarkable.

In a letter, Paul described his home: "It is a three story brick with seven rooms, with pretty alcoves on the upper floors and with all modern improvements." According to *Lyrics of Sunshine and Shadow: The Tragic Courtship and Marriage of Paul Laurence Dunbar and Alice Ruth Moore* (2001) by Eleanor Alexander: "Their marriage was a public one, due to Paul's renown. It was treated in the press as a great love story, despite evidence that Paul was an alcoholic who beat her regularly, abused her verbally, and violated her sexually." Then "an inebriated Paul physically assaulted Alice on January 25, 1902, and according to his friend T. Thomas Fortune, tried to kill her. Alice confirmed the allegation: 'He came home one night in a beastly condition.

I went to him to help him to bed—and he behaved . . . disgracefully. He left that night, and I was ill for weeks with peritonitis brought on by his kicks.' In pre-penicillin America at the turn of the twentieth century, peritonitis could be a deadly disorder."

Foreshadowing this incident, the author emphasizes "a November night in 1897, during their engagement period, [when] Paul, in a drunken state, raped Alice, leaving her with internal injuries requiring medical treatment." She also writes of "evidence demonstrating that Paul had gonorrhea at the time, and in all probability, infected Alice."

Both Paul and Alice were the children of former slaves, members of the first generation of free and educated people of color, and both had to overcome a youth in poverty to become published authors. The tenuousness of their social position as part of a rising group of African American elites made them very socially conservative. This played out in their ideals of beauty (the shades of skin closer to white—such as her complexion—were favored over darker skin, like his), their gender roles (she was expected to be the subservient and meek wife who did not work outside the home), and their conceptions and expectations of romantic love. Paul expected Alice to put up with his mood swings, as well as his excessive drinking, his spending beyond his means, and his affairs with other women.

➔ **Retrace your steps and take the first left onto U Street.**

8 Site of the Second Dunbar House

321 U Street NW

The Dunbars' second DC home was described by Benjamin Brawley: "On the floors were Navajo rugs brought from the West, and here and there the skin of an animal stretched before an easy chair. The walls of the study were adorned with posters, some of Kemble's drawings, and the portraits of other authors. Below were bookshelves, and in a special case copies of the poet's works, and numerous autographed volumes."

Paul wrote: "I am afraid the climate of Washington does not suit me . . . but there is much to hold me here. The best Negroes in the country find their way to the capital, and I have a very congenial and delightful circle of friends."

Upper-class African Americans in DC around the turn of the twentieth century came together in churches, public concerts and lectures, and in private clubs. Paul was an active member of two men's clubs, the Bachelor-Benedict Club and the exclusive Pen and Pencil Club. Alice attended the Monday Night Literary Society, a women's reading group.

Paul worked as an assistant in the reading room of the Library of Congress, a job that paid a salary of $720 a year. Such prestigious white-collar jobs were rare. According to *Paul Laurence Dunbar: Poet of His People* (1936), by Benjamin Brawley: "He remained at the Library for fifteen months, until the end of 1898, by which time his writing was better able to support him. Naturally to one of his temperament it was not congenial to be confined sometimes for hours in the stacks with scientific works. In the torrid days of midsummer the iron gratings seemed to him like the bars of a prison, especially when he came out and looked upon the inviting green of the Capitol grounds."

Paul was supervised by Daniel Alexander Payne Murray, a remarkable archivist, librarian, and bibliophile who worked at the Library of Congress for more than fifty years beginning in 1871 at age eighteen (and only the second African American hired in a professional position by that institution). After ten years, Murray was promoted to assistant librarian. In that position, he became one of the most recognized authorities on literature by people of African descent during his lifetime. His accomplishments include curation of an exhibit, *Negro Literature,* for the 1900 Paris Exposition, and a detailed bibliography of books and pamphlets compiled for the Library of Congress of works by U.S., Caribbean, and African writers of color, and writings on the subject of race.

Murray and his wife, Anna Evans Murray, lived nearby at 934 S Street NW with their seven children. Murray was the first African American to serve on the DC Board of Trade and was twice a delegate for the Republication National Convention. "In 1897," Murray wrote, "Mr. Dunbar was made an assistant to me that he might learn library methods and have, at the same time, one who would take an interest in his advancement. The late Colonel Robert Ingersoll was largely responsible for his taking the position, believing that it would afford him an opportunity to acquire information that could be turned to account in his literary career." (This is the same man who gave the funeral oration for Walt Whitman.)

In two essays on Negro life in Washington that he published in 1900 and 1901, Dunbar described the city as the place where "the breeziness of the West" met "the refinement of the East, the warmth and grace of the South," and "the culture and fine reserve of the North."

The "social life of the Negro," he argued, was more highly developed in Washington than in any other city in the country and could no longer be "laughed at or caricatured under the name of 'colored sassiety.'" Class lines were "strictly drawn," and one from outside DC would be no more likely to gain admission to the "black 400" without "a perfect knowledge of his standing in his own community than would Mrs. Bradley Martin's butler to an Astor ball." It was therefore not surprising, Dunbar remarked, that some African Americans "wince a bit when we are thrown into a lump with the peasant or serving class."

"In aims and hopes for our race," he concluded, "we are all as one, but it must be understood that when we come to consider the social life, the girls who cook in your kitchens and the men who serve in your dining rooms do not dance in your parlors."

9 Site of the Christian A. and Sara Iredell Fleetwood House

319 U Street NW

The Fleetwoods were among the African American elite's first families in DC. Major Christian Fleetwood was among a group of thirteen men who were the first African Americans to be awarded the Medal of Honor by the U.S. Congress. Fleetwood was honored for his heroism during the Civil War at the Battle of Chaffin's Farm near Richmond, Virginia, while serving in the U.S. Colored Volunteer Army.

Major Fleetwood, born free, was a graduate of Ashmun University (a forerunner to Lincoln University) who worked as a clerk at Freedman's Savings and Trust Company, then for three decades at the War Department. He also instructed the Colored Washington High School Cadet Corps and helped organize DC's first African American National Guard unit.

Sara Fleetwood married the major in 1869. She was a graduate of the first nursing school class at Freedmen's Hospital and became the first African American superintendent of nurses at that hospital in 1901.

The major was a fine musician and choirmaster, organizing the American Orchestra Club to perform concerts at DC churches. Mrs. Fleetwood hosted weekly literary gatherings every Thursday, which she called "Evenings at Home."

The two were also active in charitable works. During the 1893 depression, the Fleetwoods helped organize other well-to-do African American families to donate funds to purchase and dispense coal, food, clothing, and other supplies. The Fleetwoods were living at that time slightly north of here, at 2230 Sixth Street (an address now part of the Howard University campus); the Fleetwood home became a hub for the storage and dispersal of donated goods.

The couple lived at this address from the 1890s until Mrs. Fleetwood's death in 1908. The major moved in with a daughter until his own death six years later.

➔ **Go to the end of the block.**

10 Lucy Diggs Slowe Hall, Howard University

1919 Third Street NW

Slowe Hall was the site of Duke Ellington's first home as a newlywed in 1918. He lived at this location with his new wife, Edna Thompson Ellington, for one year.

Houses along this block were razed during World War II to erect this building for single women of color working for the federal government. The war years saw a huge influx of new government workers and a resulting housing shortage. This dormitory was one of several built in DC to address that problem. After the war, the building was transformed into a hotel that catered to foreign dignitaries who, according to a real estate handbook of the time, "being of a complexion hue, cannot secure accommodations in the down-town hotels."

The building was purchased by Howard University in 1948 for use as off-campus student housing. At that time the name was changed to Lucy Diggs Slowe Hall.

The first dean of women at Howard University, Slowe was an administrator at Howard for fifteen years and created and led two national professional associations of college administrators, the National Association of College Women, and the Association of Advisors to Women in Colored Schools. She was one of the founders of the Alpha Kappa Alpha sorority. She was also became the first African American woman to win a major sports title when she won the American Tennis Association's first tournament in 1917. In addition to having a residence hall at Howard named in her honor, a DC public elementary school was named for her (now part of the Mary McLeod Bethune Day Academy Public Charter School). She is considered one of the most important advocates for women's education and self-determination in the first half of the twentieth century. She lived in the Brookland neighborhood with her life partner, the playwright and educator Mary P. Burrill.

In 2017, the university sold this property to private developers; they plan to convert the building to condominiums.

→ **Turn left onto Third Street.**

11 General William Birney House

1901 Third Street NW

Only two of the original McGill-designed homes remain on what is now known as Anna J. Cooper Memorial Circle, and they were the homes of the Civil War general William Birney and his son Arthur, a law professor at Howard University. Both were white.

General Birney is notable as an ardent abolitionist who organized seven regiments of free African American men for the Union army. In 1863, he was appointed one of three superintendents of colored enlistments. He was named colonel of the Twenty-Second U.S. Colored Troops. Later that year, he was promoted to brigadier general and assigned to recruit free blacks in Maryland. He participated in battles at Bull Run, Chantilly, Fredericksburg, Chancellorsville, Chaffin's Farm, Richmond, Petersburg (where he was promoted again, this time to brevet major general), and Appomattox.

After the war, he lived for several years in Florida, then moved to DC in 1874 to open a law practice. He served as U.S. attorney for the District of Columbia, and lived at this address until his death in 1907. He is buried in Oak Hill Cemetery in Georgetown.

Anna Julia Cooper House in LeDroit Park

→ **At the circle, turn left onto T Street.**

12 Anna Julia Cooper House

201 T Street NW

Cooper is the author of *A Voice from the South* (1892), a collection of essays widely considered the earliest book of African American feminism. Cooper taught and was principal at M Street High School, and later Freling-huysen University. When she earned her PhD from the Sorbonne in 1924, she became the fourth African American woman with a doctoral degree.

Cooper was born a slave. She married, but her husband died after just two years, and she never remarried. In 1915, her half brother died, and she adopted his five children, raising them on her own.

Cooper was in demand as an orator, and some of her most famous speeches were given at the World's Congress of Representative Women (Chicago, 1893) and the Pan-African Congress (London, 1900). She helped organize the Colored Women's League of Washington, the Colored Settlement House, and the DC Colored Young Women's Christian Association.

Cooper lived to the age of 105. Among the twelve famous Americans quoted in U.S. passports, she is the only woman. Her quote: "The cause of freedom is not the cause of a race or a sect, a party or a class—it is the cause of humankind, the very birthright of humanity."

➜ **Go back to the circle, and walk around to continue walking east on T Street.**

13 Robert and Mary Church Terrell House

326 T Street NW

Robert H. Terrell was the first African American municipal judge in the District of Columbia. A graduate of Harvard University and Howard University Law School, he had difficulty at first getting a job as an African American attorney, so between 1884 and 1891, he taught in the DC Public Schools, where he met his wife, who also taught there. He then worked as chief clerk in the office of the auditor of the U.S. Treasury. From 1892 to 1898, Robert practiced law, but he returned to teaching to become principal of M Street High School. In 1910, he was appointed a judge over the bitter opposition of southern Democrats in the Senate. He served as a municipal judge until his death in 1925. While a judge, he was also on the faculty of the Howard University Law School.

Mary Church Terrell is best known as an activist working for civil rights and women's rights. She served on the DC Board of Education from 1895 to 1906, the first African American woman in the nation to hold such a position. Molly, as she was known, was president of the National Association of Colored Women's Clubs, and cofounded the National Association of College Women. In 1909, she became a founding member of the National Association for the Advancement of Colored People. She was an organizer for the women's suffrage movement after World War I and led the fight to integrate restaurants in DC in 1950.

Terrell's journalism was published widely in both the white and black press, in such publications as the *Afro-American, New York Age, Washington Tribune, Washington Evening Star,* and *Washington Post.*

Molly also lectured extensively, touring under the auspices of the Slayton Lyceum Bureau from 1895 to 1910. According to *Leading the Race: The Transformation of the Black Elite in the Nation's Capital, 1880–1920* (1999) by Jacqueline M. Moore:

Terrell's stock speeches reveal her dedication to the spirit of uplift. In "The Bright Side of a Dark Subject," Terrell discussed the progress of the race and stressed the positive rather than dwelling on what still needed reform. In "The Progress of Colored Women," she recounted charitable works accomplished by black women, particularly through the NACW and church clubs. She also discussed the intellectual achievements of black women in the nation's colleges and obstacles they were required to overcome. By nature a feminist, Terrell stressed the fact that black women had two burdens to bear, those of race and those of sex. In "Uncle Sam and the Sons of Ham," she described forthrightly the attitude of the government toward race relations and examined disfranchisement and the convict lease system.

In her autobiography, *A Colored Woman in a White World* (1940), Mary Church Terrell wrote:

When Paul Dunbar married he brought his wife and his mother to live in my father's house, which was next door to ours. Precious memories rush over me like a flood every time I pass that house. I can see Paul Dunbar beckoning me, as I walked by, when he wanted to read me a poem which he had just written or when he wished to discuss a word or a subject on which he had not fully decided. Paul often came to see me to read his poems or his prose articles before he sent them to magazines. Sometimes he would tauntingly wave back and forth a check which he had just received and say, "Wouldn't you like to see that?" then, after he thought he had aroused my curiosity sufficiently, he would show it to me and say, "Now, look quick. Don't keep it long. Give it back to me right away."

➜ **Continue west on T Street.**

14 LeDroit Park Gateway

In an interview, Dunbar said:

When I first began my career, I wrote rapidly, accomplishing without difficulty five thousand words a day. Now I write slowly—oh! so slowly. I sometimes spend three weeks on a chapter and then am not satisfied with the result. Indeed, I have never yet succeeded in perfectly reproducing what was in my mind. Fortunately for the artist, however, the public doesn't see the mental picture, and the poor copy isn't favorably contrasted. Indeed, my work becomes harder, rather than easier, as I go on, simply because I am more critical of it. I believe when an author ceases to climb, he ceases at the same time to lift his readers up with him.

Paul returned to Dayton, Ohio, in 1903, living in a house with his mother until his early death in 1906 from tuberculosis, at the age of thirty-three. Even while in declining health, he wrote and published prolifically. Although he and Alice were separated, they never divorced. No one, however, notified her when Paul was dying. She read about his death in a Wilmington, Delaware, newspaper, while riding a streetcar.

Alice had moved from DC to Delaware to live with her mother and sister and her sister's four children, and both sisters taught at Howard High School in Wilmington. Alice became active in Republican Party politics, worked for suffrage, and was a journalist. She would marry two more times: to Henry Arthur Callis and to Robert J. Nelson. Her third marriage was her happiest. For the rest of her life, she continued to collect royalties from the book sales of her first husband. Her use of his name, and her status as his widow, helped her continue to secure publications, lectures, and renown.

The accomplishments of these two talented and remarkable writers came against a backdrop of rapidly changing social times. One generation removed from slavery, they moved to DC the year after the U.S. Supreme Court ruled in *Plessy v. Ferguson,* making "separate but equal" public accommodations legal across the United States, segregating people of color from whites and inaugurating a new, dark era of lynching, convict labor, sharecropping, voter suppression, and other brutal and regressive policies throughout the South.

Reconstruction ended officially in 1877 with the removal of federal troops from the former Confederate states. As Elizabeth Dowling Taylor writes in *The Original Black Elite: Daniel Murray and the Story of a Forgotten Era* (2017):

The national government not only revoked its commitment to black advancement but delivered its new citizens into the hands of white supremacists, who lost no time in renewing their oppression. . . . the lynching of blacks increased steadily through the 1880s and 1890s . . . but not even murder-by-mob led the federal government to abandon its policy of noninterference in southern affairs.

Although DC was considered much more progressive than other southern cities, by 1878, Congress had removed home rule from residents and replaced it with federal oversight. Carol Gelderman writes in *A Free Man of Color and His Hotel: Race, Reconstruction, and the Role of the Federal Government* (2012):

The Act of 1878 stipulated that Congress would govern the federal area with three presidentially approved commissioners serving as executives, and, in return for the denial of any local say about taxes and other local problems, the federal government would share expenses equally with District taxpayers. The commissioners would appoint the police, a school board, and a health officer. The president would also name the justices of the District Supreme Court. Negroes had made greater strides in Washington than anywhere else in the United States, but this act, which abruptly disenfranchised native Washingtonians, ended political associations between Negroes and whites.

Yet Paul Dunbar's assertive voice broke through. His poems inspired generations of African Americans, and he was a crossover sensation with white readers as well. Paul's popular "dialect poems" were controversial among people of color even in his own time, but they have recently generated new interest among scholars. He wrote both in dialect and in Standard English, seeking new ways to express what made African American experience distinct. Both his work and Alice's less-well-known writing deserve a continued following. The characters they created are filled with joy and dignity, and they are complex and compelling enough to reward continued rereading.

Poems by Paul Laurence Dunbar and Alice Dunbar-Nelson

According to Alice Dunbar-Nelson, writing years after Paul's death, his poem "Lover's Lane" was inspired by walks the two made down what was then called Spruce Street (now U Street) in LeDroit Park: "The white arc light of the corner lamp, filtering through the arches of the maples on Spruce Street, make for the tender suggestion in 'Lover's Lane,' where the lovers walk side by side under the 'shadder-mekin' trees."

This poem is also a fine example of the "dialect" poems for which Dunbar was so widely praised by mainstream white audiences.

LOVER'S LANE

Paul Laurence Dunbar

Summah night an' sighin' breeze,
'Long de lovah's lane;

Frien'ly, shadder-mekin' trees,
'Long de lovah's lane.

White folks' wo'k all done up gran'—
Me an' 'Mandy han'-in-han'
Struttin' lak we owned de lan',
'Long de lovah's lane.

Owl a-settin' 'side de road,
Long de lovah's lane,
Lookin' at us lak he knowed
Dis uz lovah's lane.

Go on, hoot yo' mou'nful tune,
You ain' nevah loved in June,
An' come hidin' f'om de moon
Down in lovah's lane.

Bush it ben' an' nod an' sway,
Down in lovah's lane,
Try'n' to hyeah me whut I say
'Long de lovah's lane.

But I whispahs low lak dis,
An' my 'Mandy smile huh bliss—
Mistah Bush he shek his fis',
Down in lovah's lane.

Whut I keer ef day is long,
Down in lovah's lane.
I kin allus sing a song
'Long de lovah's lane.

An' de wo'ds I hyeah an' say
Meks up fu' de weary day
W'en I's strollin' by de way,
Down in lovah's lane.

An' dis t'ought will allus rise
Down in lovah's lane;
Wondah whethah in de skies
Dey's a lovah's lane.

Ef dey ain't, I tell you true,
'Ligion do look mighty blue,
'Cause I do' know whut I'd do
'Dout a lovah's lane.

Dunbar sometimes wrote of his wife metaphorically, using her favorite flower, the violet, as a stand-in. Here is a poem by Dunbar-Nelson, in response:

SONNET

Alice Moore Dunbar-Nelson

I had not thought of violets late,
The wild, shy kind that spring beneath your feet
In wistful April days, when lovers mate
And wander through the fields in raptures sweet.
The thought of violets meant florists' shops,
And cabarets and soaps, and deadening wines.
So far from sweet real things my thoughts had strayed,
I had forgot wide fields; and clear brown streams;
The perfect loveliness that God has made,—
Wild violets shy and Heaven-mounting dreams.
And now—unwittingly, you've made me dream
Of violets, and my soul's forgotten gleam.

Portraits

Frederick Douglass

February 1818?–February 20, 1895

It is not light that we need, but fire; it is not the gentle shower, but thunder. We need the storm, the whirlwind, and the earthquake.

Social reformer, statesman, powerful orator, and writer, Frederick Douglass was born a slave in Talbot County, Maryland, and became a leader in the abolitionist movement and the women's rights movement. From 1889 to 1891, he was consul-general to the Republic of Haiti.

His memoirs include *A Narrative of the Life of Frederick Douglass, an American Slave* (1845), *My Bondage and My Freedom* (1855), and *Life and Times of Frederick Douglass* (1881, revised 1892). These books were written, "sincerely and earnestly hoping . . . [to] do something toward throwing light on the American slave system, and hastening the glad day of deliverance to the millions of my brethren in bonds—faithfully relying upon the power of truth, love, and justice, for success in my humble efforts—and solemnly pledging myself anew to the sacred cause."

Douglass moved to DC in 1872 and purchased Cedar Hill in 1877. His house and its contents are now preserved by the National Park Service. Visitors can see his library with his desk and books and view a re-creation of his private studio in the backyard, which he called The Growlery. The studio is a thick-walled single-room

Frederick Douglass

building constructed of rough stones, with no windows to distract him as he worked.

While living in DC, Douglass was an editor for the abolitionist newspaper *New National Era,* and served as a U.S. marshal and as DC recorder of deeds. He also served on the Board of Trustees of Howard University, was appointed to the city's Legislative Council, advocated for DC suffrage, and raised money for the Negro Division of the DC Public Schools. He was a regular speaker at churches and invested money in the city's first streetcar line.

Cedar Hill, located at 1411 W Street NW, is perched on a prominent knoll with sweeping views across the Anacostia River to the U.S. Capitol. Douglass lived in this house with his wife of forty years, Anna Murray Douglass, and then, after her death and his remarriage, with Helen Pitts Douglass. Helen Douglass was a white woman more than forty years his junior who had worked for Douglass at the DC Recorder of Deeds office, and this second marriage was controversial. He had five children with his first wife, four of whom lived to adulthood.

Other properties he owned in DC still stand, at 2000–2004 Seventeenth Street NW and 320 A Street NE. Douglass is remembered locally by a bridge across the Anacostia River named in his honor. A statue of Douglass created by Steven Weitzman was added to National Statuary Hall in the U.S. Capitol, representing the District of Columbia, in 2013.

In 1875, Douglass gave a speech titled "A Lecture on Our National Capitol." The speech is unusual for its use of humor, but it also has plenty of Douglass's trademark earnestness, which made his speeches so thrilling and inspiring to his audiences. It is worth quoting at length:

No American now has a skin too dark to call Washington his home, and no American now has a skin so white and a heart so black as to deny him that right. Under the majestic dome of the American Capitol, as truly as under the broad blue sky of heaven, men of all races, colors, and conditions may now stand in equal freedom, thrilled with the sentiment of equal citizenship and common country. The wealth, beauty, and magnificence which, if seen elsewhere, might oppress the lowly with a sad sense of their personal insignificance, seen here, ennoble them to their own eyes and are felt to be only fit and proper to the capital of a great nation. . . .

Justice is not always found on the bench, nor purity in the pulpit, nor saints at the altar. It will not do to assume for Washington either moral or material preeminence over other cities of the Union. On the contrary, Washington, as compared with many other parts of the country, has been, and still is, a most disgraceful and scandalous contradiction to the march of civilization. . . .

I would do injustice in the matter of the population of Washington if I failed to say a word of another element in the social composition of the Capital . . . the spoilsmen of every grade and description. They are the officeholders, officeseekers, contract buyers, pension agents, lobbyists, commissioners, and run-betweens in general. Men are here with all sorts of schemes and enterprises. . . . Nowhere will you find a greater show of insincere politeness. The very air is vexed with clumsy compliments and obsequious hatlifting.

Everybody wants a favor; everybody expects favor; everybody is looking for favor; everybody is afraid of losing favor; hence everybody knows the full value and quality of this general self-abasement. You will seldom hear an honest, square, upright, and downright *no* in all this eager and hungry crowd. . . . The National Capital is never without a fair representation of these hungry spoilsmen, but the incoming of a new administration is the signal for the gathering in force of this remorseless class. The avenues of the city and the corridors of the Capitol and of other public buildings are the literal whirlpools of social driftwood from every section of the Republic.

Its members are met with in all directions. They are crowding, elbowing, and buttonholing, everywhere.

The least offensive of this multitude are those who come here to obtain clerkships and other positions in the several government departments. There is nothing in this service to degrade or to demoralize, and yet I cannot recommend any young man to seek this mode of livelihood. . . .

It is commonly thought to be a nice and pleasant thing to be a member of Congress, but I think it would be difficult for a man to find any position more abundant in vexation. A man who gets himself elected to Congress can seldom do so without drawing after him to Washington a lively swarm of political creditors who want their pay in the shape of an office somewhere in the Civil Service. They besiege his house at all hours, night and day, break his bell wires before breakfast, and so crowd his doorway that, if he is in, he cannot get out without seeing them, and if he is out, he cannot get in without seeing them. They waylay him as he goes to his house and dog him to the very doors and summon him to the cloakroom or lobby after he may have been so fortunate as to have reached his seat in the House of Representatives.

In all this sort of vexation and trouble he must be too polite or too prudent to express the slightest sense of annoyance. If he would be a successful politician he must face it all with blandest suavity and the patience of a true martyr.

But members of Congress are not the only victims of this incessant, persistent, and annoying importunity to help to get official positions. The hour a man takes up his abode in Washington, his relation to the administration is inquired into and ascertained. No neutrality is allowed him. He is instantly weighed, measured, and stamped, and duly assigned to one of two classes: the class which is used by everybody or the class that uses everybody.

Once let it get abroad that you are friendly to the administration, or worse still, that the administration is friendly to you, and you will at once find yourself a famous man. Smiling faces anxious to see you and to serve their country will cluster and whirl about your pathway, like the ripe leaves of a declining autumn. If you were never before aware of your greatness, you will be made aware of it now, as plain as words can reveal it. Men will tell you of it oftener than you can muster face to hear it. You will be urged to sign papers, write letters, and go in person and urge the appointment of some one of your numerous friends and admirers, every day in the year, and if you do not *sign, write,* and *go,* you will be denounced as a cold and heartless man.

I have had, since residing in Washington, my full share of this kind of service. I am usually approached by the dark side of our fellow citizens. They have been told by somebody, somewhere, that if they can only get to Washington and find Douglass, they will be quite sure to get an office.

When white men wish my aid they tell me wonderful things of what they or their fathers did in the abolition cause, when it cost something to be known as an abolitionist. Through this class I have learned that there were a great many more Underground Railroad Stations at the North than I ever dreamed of in the time of slavery and when I sorely needed one myself.

Just what becomes of this ever-accumulating and ever-dissolving cloud of place hunters, I cannot engage to tell.

Like the mist and spray which rises over the cataract of Niagara, its particles are ever meeting and separating in the air. One goes, another comes, and none stay long. Few are successful in getting what they seek. There are a hundred applicants for every ten vacancies. . . .

A very brief acquaintance will convince one that Congress is not the place for either a vain man or a weak man. He may be a very great man at home and a very small man in Congress. It is one thing to be weighed and measured by one's friends, neighbors, and admirers, but quite another thing to be measured in comparison with the chosen representatives of forty millions of people. In this presence your weak man will easily sink to nothingness, and your vain man, if not hopelessly blind and insensible, will have his vanity completely taken out of him. He will be allowed to pass in a crowd but will find no admiring eyes feasting upon his fine face, his fine figure, or his fine clothing. The people there gathered are accustomed to hear and see great men. They are experts: they know at a glance the genuine from the spurious, the false from the true, the sheet-iron thunder of the stage from the royal thunder of heaven.

Frances Hodgson Burnett

November 24, 1849–October 29, 1924

Although best known now as the author of children's books, Frances Hodgson Burnett started out as a novelist for adults. In 1877, soon after the publication of her first book, *That Lass o' Lowries,* she moved to DC, where she joined her first husband, a medical doctor who was setting up a new practice in the city. Burnett quickly established a reputation as a rising novelist and society hostess, and she held a literary salon in her home near Dupont Circle on Tuesday evenings, drawing local writers and politicians. That house, which once stood in the 1700 block of Massachusetts Avenue NW, was where Burnett lived from 1877 until her divorce in 1898, some of her most productive years as a writer.

The author of more than forty books, Burnett's reputation today rests on two books for children, *The Secret Garden* (1911) and *Little Lord Fauntleroy* (1885). She was the mother of two sons, one of whom died of tuberculosis; her memoir, *The One I Knew Best of All* (1893) documents that loss. She married and divorced twice, which was considered scandalous in her time. Burnett also struggled with depression, and after her

Frances Hodgson Burnett

son Lionel's death, she embraced Christian Science and forms of spiritualism.

Among her fiction and plays, she authored: *Louisiana* (1880), *Little Saint Elizabeth, and Other Stories* (1893), *A Lady of Quality* (1896), *The Making of a Marchioness* (1901), *Queen Silver-Bell* (1906), and *The Lost Prince* (1915). One of her most popular novels for adults, *Through One Administration* (1883), charts the courtship of a military hero of the Indian Wars with a DC society belle, while commenting on the dangers of political corruption. Three short excerpts from the book are reprinted here.

He had arrived only a day or so after the occurrence of an event of no less national importance than the inauguration of a newly elected President, and there still remained traces of the festivities attendant upon this ceremony, in the shape of unremoved decorations fluttering from windows, draping doors, and swaying in lines across the streets. Groups of people, wearing a rather fatigued air of having remained after the feast for the purpose of more extended sight-seeing, gave the sidewalks a well-filled look, and here and there among them was to be seen a belated uniform which had figured effectively in the procession to the Capitol two days before. Having taken note of these things, Tredennis leaned back upon his musty cushions with a half sigh of weariness. "I come in with the Administration," he said. "I wonder if I shall go out with it, and what will have happened in the interval." . . .

It was the rule, and not the exception, that in walking out he met persons he knew or knew of, and he found it at no time difficult to discover the names and positions of those who attracted his attention. Almost all noticeable and numerous unnoticeable persons were to be distinguished in some way from their fellows. The dark, sinewy man he observed standing on the steps of a certain family hotel was a noted New England senator; his companion was the head of an important department; the man who stood near was the private secretary of the President, or the editor of one of the dailies, or a man with a much-discussed claim against the Government; the handsome woman whose carriage drew up before a fashionable millinery establishment the wife of a foreign diplomat, or of a well-known politician, or of a member of the Cabinet; the woman who crossed her path as she got out was a celebrated female suffragist, or female physician, or lawyer, or perhaps that much-talked of will-o'-the-wisp, a female lobbyist; and eight persons out of every ten passing them knew their names and not a little of their private history. So much was crowded within a comparatively limited radius that it was not easy for any person or thing worthy of note to be lost or hidden from the public eye. . . .

It was New-Year's day, and His Excellency the President had had several months in which to endeavor to adjust himself to the exigencies of his position; though whether he had accomplished this with a result of entire satisfaction to himself and all parties concerned and unconcerned, had, perhaps unfortunately, not been a matter of record. According to a time-honored custom, he had been placed at the slight disadvantage of being called upon to receive, from time to time, the opinions of the nation concerning himself without the opportunity of expressing, with any degree of publicity, his own opinions regarding the nation. . . . Every event of his political career and domestic life had been held up to public derision, laudation, and criticism. It had been successfully proved that his education had been entirely neglected, and that his advantages had been marvelous; that he had read Greek at the tender age of four years, and that he had not learned to read at all until he attained his majority; that his wife had taught him his letters, and that he had taught his wife to spell; that he was a liar, a forger, and a thief; that he was a model of virtue, probity, and honor, each and all of which incontrovertible facts had been public property and a source of national pride and delight. . . .

There had descended upon the newly elected ruler an avalanche of seekers for office, a respectable number of whom laid in his hands the future salvation of their souls and bodies, and generously left to him the result. He found himself suddenly established as the guardian of the widow, the orphan, and the friendless, and required to repair fortunes or provide them, as the case might be, at a moment's notice; his sympathies were appealed to, his interests, his generosity, as an altogether omnipotent power in whose hands all things lay, and whose word was naturally law upon all occasions, great or small; and any failure on his part to respond to the entirely reasonable requests preferred was very properly laid to a tendency to abandoned scheming or to the heartless indifference of the great. . . .

On this particular New Year's day there were few traces on the social surface of the disasters which so short a time before had threatened to engulf all. Washington wore an aspect even gayer than usual. The presidential reception began the day in its most imposing manner. Lines of carriages thronged the drive before the White House, and the diplomatists, statesmen, officials, and glittering beings in naval and military uniform, who descended from them, were possibly cheered and encouraged by the comments of the lookers-on, who knew them and their glories and their shortcomings by heart.

The Gilded Age, 1870–1910

Henry Adams

Henry Adams in Lafayette Square

This walking tour captures the lives of elite white writers during what came to be known as the Gilded Age. It focuses on the most famous of a group of writers who lived and worked around Lafayette Square at that time: Henry Adams.

Adams first visited Washington, DC, in 1850 when he was twelve; his father, Charles Francis Adams, was a Republican congressman from Massachusetts and brought him to visit his grandmother Louisa Adams, who was then living on F Street NW. At the earliest glimpse of the city, Henry fell in love. He wrote: "The want of barriers, of pavements, of forms, the looseness, the laziness; the indolent southern drawl; the pigs in the streets; the Negro babies, and their mothers with bandanas; the freedom, openness, swagger of nature and man, soothed."

He next returned at age twenty-one in the capacity of his father's personal secretary, after Lincoln's election in 1860, and stayed just a few months. When Senator Adams was appointed ambassador to the United Kingdom, Henry continued to work for his father in London during the Civil War years and after (from 1861 to 1868). From 1868 to 1870, Henry lived once again in Washington, working as a journalist. From 1870 to 1877, he lived in Boston, Massachusetts, and worked at

Walking Tour 3: Henry Adams in Lafayette Square

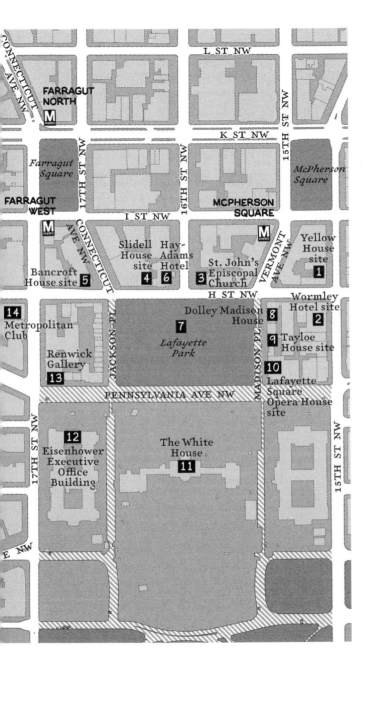

Harvard College as a professor of medieval history and as editor of the *North American Review*.

He married Marian Hooper, known to friends as Clover, in 1872. Clover came from a prominent and wealthy Boston family. She was clever, outspoken, with a dazzling wit and a sharp tongue. She wrote that Adams was "utterly devoted" to her. They were unable to have children.

When Henry retired from Harvard at age thirty-nine, he moved to Washington to become a full-time historian and writer. He lived in the capital until his death at age eighty, in 1918.

→ **Start at the McPherson Square Metro Station. Walk one block south on Fifteenth Street.**

1 Site of the Yellow House (now a hotel)

1501 H Street NW

Adams lived here from 1877 to 1880. Of his decision to move back to Washington after relinquishing his teaching career, he wrote: "This is the only place in America where society amuses me, or where life offers variety." In a letter, he said, "One of these days this will be a very great city if nothing happens to it. Even now it is a beautiful one, and its situation is superb."

Adams enjoyed the mix of society and politics, and in the mornings, he rode a horse almost daily in Rock Creek Park, where he could enjoy dogwood, flowering Judas, rhododendron, and hepatica. He wrote rapturously, "The Potomac and its tributaries squandered beauty" with their "intermixture of delicate grace and passionate depravity." Clover oversaw a household staff of four servants (later increased to six), and they owned two Skye terriers named Boojum and Pollywog.

While living in this location, Adams wrote a biography, *The Life of Albert Gallatin* (1879), and edited the three-volume *Writings of Albert Gallatin* (1879). Albert Gallatin, the longest-serving U.S. secretary of the Treasury, was also a foreign diplomat, founder of New York University, and a linguist who studied Native American languages. Adams wrote the first biography of the man, still considered the definitive work.

Gallatin's son asked Adams to undertake the work and made his father's personal papers available. His friend William Evarts, the new secretary of state under President Rutherford B. Hayes, offered Adams a private desk and free access to the (normally restricted) archives of the State Department.

Adams also wrote his novel *Democracy* (1880) while living here. Published anonymously, it caused a sensation in both the United States and Great Britain. In the novel, set mostly on Lafayette Square, James G. Blaine (later President James A. Garfield's secretary of state and one of Adams's neighbors) was the model for the villain, Silas P. Ratcliffe. The book is a delightful satire of American politics. Its heroine, Mrs. Lightfoot Lee, lives in a house on Lafayette Square, where she can best observe "the great American mystery of democracy and government." The book was extremely popular, and its authorship was the subject of much speculation. Adams was revealed as the author only after his death.

From 1879 until he moved, this house was the gathering place, almost daily, for afternoon teas among an extraordinary group of friends who called themselves the "Five of Hearts." Membership was limited to Henry and Clover Adams, John and Clara Hay, and Clarence King.

2 Site of the Wormley Hotel (now the American Bar Association Building)

SW corner of Fifteenth & H Streets NW

Considered one of the top hotels in DC in the postwar years, Wormley's was owned and operated by an African American family and served an exclusive, white, upper-class clientele. The hotel was renowned for its fine dining, impeccable service, and large wine cellar.

Adams lived here for two months in 1880 while William Corcoran prepared Slidell House for him; Clarence King and John Hay were also living at the hotel at the time. Adams had met both previously, but they reconnected here, and their friendship would last for the rest of all their lives.

When the Adamses moved out of Wormley's, King and Hay decided to rent a house together at 1400 Massachusetts Avenue NW, now razed, on Thomas Circle. They called it their "bachelor castle." King, fresh from his success completing the Fortieth Parallel Survey (later to be the route of the transcontinental railroad), was the first director of the U.S. Geological Survey. The two men walked part of the way to work together each morning and met again each day at 5:00 p.m. for tea with the Adamses.

Clarence King's office was at 801 G Street NW, currently the site of the Family Research Council, across the street from the Smithsonian American Art Museum (which was, at that time, the U.S. Patent Office). Adams idolized King, with his rough-and-tumble stories of western exploration. King's book *Mountaineering in the Sierra Nevada* (1871) was a scientific and commercial success.

But King was unable to live up to his friend's great expectations of him. He invested heavily in mines that did not succeed, and both Adams's and Hay's gifts of money kept him afloat in his later years. He died penniless, and after his death, he left an additional surprise: from 1888 until his death (from tuberculosis in 1901), he was the common-law husband to an African American woman in New York, with whom he had five children. Adams and Hay joked about King's mysterious and sudden absences, but they had no clue that the man they thought of as a roving bachelor was in fact happily married.

King maintained a double life, living as a working-class black man named James Todd with his wife, Ada Todd, while simultaneously keeping up his club memberships and connections in the upper-class white world. Although King appeared white, with light skin and closely cropped blond hair, Ada and his family assumed that he was of mixed heritage. He revealed his true identity to his wife in a deathbed letter.

Adams based his character George Strong, in his novel *Esther* (1884), on Clarence King. Strong is described as

an intelligent man, with a figure made for action, an eye
that hated rest, and a manner naturally sympathetic.
His forehead was so bald as to give his face a look of strong
character, which a dark beard rather helped to increase.
He was a popular fellow, known as George by whole gangs
of the roughest miners in Nevada, where he had worked
for years as a practical geologist, and it would have been
hard to find in America, Europe, or Asia, a city in which
some one would not have smiled at the mention of his
name, and asked where George was going to turn up next.

In *The Education of Henry Adams,* he wrote: "The charm of King was that he saw what others did and a great deal more. His wit and humor; his bubbling energy which swept everyone into the current of his interest; his personal charm of youth and manners; his faculty of giving and taking, profusely, lavishly, whether in thought or in money as though he were nature herself, marked him almost alone among Americans."

Considering Adams's extreme snobbery, the connection with Hay and King was a surprising one: Hay was from the Midwest, not New England, and his wife, Clara (who would move to DC to join her husband later), heiress to an industrial fortune, was shy, deeply pious, and conventional in her views.

But the Five of Hearts formed a deep bond and created an elite circle around them. As Patricia O'Toole notes in her group biography *The Five of Hearts* (1990), they "had a genius for befriending everyone worth knowing," including leading authors, intellectuals, artists, cabinet members, diplomats, and every president from Abraham Lincoln to Theodore Roosevelt. O'Toole writes that they "helped to define American culture and politics in the years between the Civil War and World War I."

➜ **Walk west on H Street.**

▣ St. John's Episcopal Church

Built in 1815–16 by Benjamin Henry Latrobe, St. John's originally had a pure, simple Greek cross design. By the time Adams lived there, subsequent additions had turned it into a more familiar (and less elegant) Latin cross with a bell tower. Traditionally considered the Church of Presidents (with the President's Pew reserved at Pew 54), St. John's is a beloved presence in Lafayette Square.

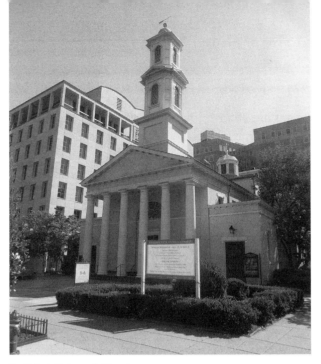

St. John's Episcopal Church

Adams was raised in the Unitarian Church but as an adult never attended any church regularly. When touring French cathedrals to write his book *Mont-Saint-Michel and Chartres* (1905), Adams became very enamored of the Catholic Marian devotions, but this emotional connection was never formalized into Catholic Church attendance. Of the Virgin Mary, Adams wrote that he was drawn to "the force of the female energy" rather than to Catholicism itself. He said that "artists constantly complained that the power embodied in a railway train could never be embodied in art. All the steam in the world could not, like the Virgin, build Chartres."

At his death, a simple funeral service was held inside Adams's home, and the rector of St. John's presided.

4 Site of Slidell House (now the U.S. Chamber of Commerce)

1607 H Street NW

Adams lived here from 1880 to 1885, renting from William Corcoran for the modest sum of two hundred dollars a month. The Adamses brought fifteen wagonloads of furniture from Boston. The house had six bedrooms, with an additional five-room servants' quarters over the stable. Originally built in 1845, an earlier tenant was Gideon Wells, Lincoln's secretary of the navy.

While living here, Adams published a biography of John Randolph (1882), his second novel, *Esther* (1884), and the first volumes of his multivolume work *History of the United States during the Administrations of Thomas Jefferson and James Madison* (1889–91).

In 1883, Adams learned that the lots next door were sold to Frederick H. Paine, who wanted to construct an apartment building on the property. Adams proposed that Hay buy out Paine, which he did in December 1883. Adams wrote to Hay: "I need not say how eager I am to spend your money to have you next door. I would sacrifice your last dollar for such an object."

Hay built two connected houses on his large lot: a mansion for himself and an adjoining smaller house for the Adamses. The Adams house, with an entrance facing Lafayette Park, was built as they ordered: "not a fine house, only an unusual one." Both Clover and Henry took great joy in watching the builders work, and Clover documented the progress with photographs. Just as it neared completion, tragedy struck. Clover's father, to whom she was extremely close, died of heart disease in 1885. Clover went into a deep depression. Henry's brother Charles wrote: "I tried to talk with her. It was painful to the last degree. She sat there pale and careworn, hardly making an effort to answer me, the very picture of physical weakness and mental depression."

In December of that year, Clover committed suicide. She poisoned herself by drinking some of her photographic chemicals. She was forty-two years old and had been happily married for twelve years.

Hay wrote to Adams: "Is it any consolation to remember her as she was? That bright, intrepid spirit, that keen, fine intellect, that lofty scorn for all that was mean, that social charm which made your house such a one as Washington never knew before and made hundreds of people love her as much as they admired her."

5 Site of Bancroft House

1623 H Street NW

George Bancroft, considered America's foremost historian, lived in a house on this site from 1874 to 1891, the last seventeen years of his life. He is the author of the ten-volume comprehensive *History of the United States* (1834–74) and the influential *History of the Formation of the Constitution of the United States* (1882). Henry and Clover Adams were frequent guests. The second floor included a four-room personal library of more than twelve thousand volumes. Bancroft also maintained a rose garden behind the house, where he cultivated more than five hundred different species and developed a new one, the American Beauty Rose.

➜ **Backtrack to the corner of H and Sixteenth Streets.**

Hay-Adams House on right, with Adams House attached on left, 1913

6 Site of Hay-Adams House (now the Hay-Adams Hotel)

800 Sixteenth Street NW

H. H. Richardson, a friend and the most prominent American architect of his day, built Adams and Hay their two adjoining houses, now the site of the Hay-Adams Hotel. John Hay was a lawyer who served as one of two personal secretaries to Lincoln (along with John Nicolay). Hay worked for a while as a journalist for the *New York Tribune,* then served as ambassador to Great Britain before becoming secretary of state to McKinley and Roosevelt. He is the coauthor (with John Nicolay) of a Lincoln biography (1890); a novel, *The Bread-Winners* (1883); a memoir, *Castilian Days* (1871); and two volumes of poetry, *Pike County Ballads* (1871) and *Poems* (1890).

Harold Dean Cater, who edited Adams's unpublished letters (1947), wrote a description of Adams's finished property:

Facing south on Lafayette Square, directly across from the White House, it was a four-storied, red-brick structure, fronting directly on the edge of the sidewalk. It had little about it that was pretentious and much that was practical. There were two broad arches on the street floor that formed bays, one of which was covered with an iron grill, and the other formed the main entrance to the house. Since the house was built in the European manner, the main living-rooms were on the floor above, and a flood of light came into them from six large south windows across the front; three were for the library and three were for Adams's study. The two top stories were used for sleeping; the lower one of the two had a recessed balcony overlooking the Square. The front stairs, designed to make climbing almost effortless, led from the street level to a hall, which in turn opened into the large library. The latter served also as a drawing-room. In this room there was a fireplace of sea-green Mexican onyx shot with red. Off the library and to the rear, was the dining-room, which had an unusual fireplace in light stone carved with wild roses. These two rooms and Adams's study opened into each other by folding doors. In all these rooms there was a sense of color and light, but a definitely masculine atmosphere.

Adams wrote, with his typical biting humor: "Richardson put back into my contract every extravagance I had struck out, and then made me sign it. After this piece of work he went off to seek other victims. He is an ogre. He devours men crude and shows the effects of inevitable indigestion in size."

The Hay-Adams House was completed in 1886, the year of Richardson's death. Adams greatly valued his friendship with Richardson, and his death, especially coming so closely upon his wife's, must have been a great loss.

The furniture in the upstairs library and study was low to the ground, specially built for Adams's short stature, and the house was filled with valuable nineteenth- and twentieth-century English paintings (oils and watercolors by such notable painters as Turner, Constable, Cotman, and Blake), drawings (by Rembrandt, Watteau, Michelangelo, and Raphael), and Japanese porcelain and sculpture in jade and bronze. Despite the seriousness of his collecting, Adams always denied that he was a connoisseur or art critic, saying, "For some things ignorance is good, and art is one of them." He left that expertise to professionals. Despite Adams's virulent anti-Semitism, his art dealer was Jewish, and Adams openly told him he was the only Jew whose company he could abide. (In private correspondence, Adams complained that Jews were "ruining" first-class accommodations for him on overseas ships.)

Adams always spent the summer months away. When Clover was still alive, they summered in Massachusetts. After her death, Adams became a more dedicated traveler, with long trips to Japan, Hawaii, the South Sea Islands, and Europe. Most of his summers were spent in Paris and London.

Adams lived on this site from just after his wife's suicide in 1885 to the end of his life in 1918. While here, he published *Historical Essays* (1891), *Mont-Saint-Michel and Chartres* (1904), *The Life of George Cabot Lodge* (1911), and the work for which he is best known, his autobiography, *The Education of Henry Adams* (1907).

When he sent a copy of *The Education* to his friend Henry James, he noted: "The volume is a mere shield of protection in the grave. I advise you to take your own life in the same way, in order to prevent biographers from taking it in theirs."

Adams had the book privately printed in a limited edition of one hundred, which he shared with friends. The book was edited and rereleased after his death, in 1918, by Houghton Mifflin Company and awarded a Pulitzer Prize. It remains a classic of American literature and has never gone out of print.

When John Hay died in 1905, his daughter Alice Hay Wadsworth inherited his house, and she bought the Adams House next door when Henry Adams died in 1917. She sold her lots to a developer, Harry Wardman, who demolished the houses in 1927 to create a luxury residence hotel. The eight-story Hay-Adams Hotel, faced in limestone with classical details, was designed by Mihran Mesrobian.

7 Lafayette Square

This famous seven-acre park was named to honor the Marquis de Lafayette, the French general who fought in the American Revolution. Statues commemorate Andrew Jackson and four Revolutionary War heroes of foreign birth.

Sarah Luria, in her book *Capital Speculations* (2006), notes: "Jackson was the man who had overthrown the Adams dynasty, banishing them to Quincy 'to eat their hearts out in disappointment and disgust.' . . . Standing literally between Adams and the White House, the Jackson statue must have continually baited Adams to settle old scores."

Ernest B. Furgurson writes in *Freedom Rising* (2004):

The rectangle around the statue, called President's Square until the visit of the Marquis de Lafayette in 1824, turned from mud to dust as the seasons changed. But appearance was not all: Henry Adams, perhaps because he lived there, would write that those seven acres were the hub of American society—"beyond the Square the country began." This was an understandable exaggeration, for even before the Civil War, such memorable characters as Dolley Madison, Stephen Decatur, Daniel Webster, Henry Clay and Jackson himself had lived in homes about the unfinished park.

In 1887, Congress appropriated funds to upgrade the park, and gravel walkways were replaced by asphalt, new benches were placed, and the lodge building at the north end was built to accommodate a night watchman, with two restrooms attached for public use (one for gentlemen and the other reserved not for women, but for nannies with children).

→ **Walk east on H Street to Madison Place NW.**

8 Cutts-Madison House and Robert G. Ingersoll House (now the Howard T. Markey National Courts Building)

In 1882, the Ingersoll House at 23 Madison Place was rented by the Cosmos Club. The club, founded by Major John Wesley Powell in 1878, was for scientific men. Henry Adams was a founding member, along with the geologist Clarence King; head of the Smithsonian Institution Spencer Baird; Johns Hopkins University president Daniel Coit Gilman; Edward Gallaudet, president of the National School for the Deaf; and others. As the membership grew, they arranged to purchase the Dolley Madison House as well. Adams was elected to the club's first Committee on Admissions.

Cutts-Madison House, constructed by Richard Cutts in 1818–19, the residence of former First Lady Dolley Madison from 1837 to 1849, home of the Cosmos Club from 1886 to 1952, now part of the Howard T. Markey National Courts Building.

The National Geographic Society was an outgrowth of the Cosmos Club, and a separate entrance was added to the clubhouse for Society members in 1891 and numbered 1518 H Street NW.

9 Site of Tayloe House (now the Howard T. Markey National Courts Building)

21 Madison Place NW

The Tayloe House was purchased in 1887 by Senator J. Donald Cameron of Pennsylvania. His second wife,

Lizzie, was the niece of General William Tecumseh Sherman and was half the age of her husband when they married. The marriage was not a happy one, and she developed a platonic love with Henry Adams after the death of his wife, Clover. Adams wrote to Hay, "I adore her, and respect the way she has kept herself out of scandal and mud, and done her duty by the lump of clay she promised to love and respect."

When a daughter was born to the Camerons two years after Clover's death, Henry Adams was ecstatic. He built a special doll house for Martha in a sliding panel in his library wall, and wrote in his journal: "By dint of incessant bribery and attentions have quite won her attachment so that she will come to me from anyone. . . . Her drawer of chocolate drops and ginger-snaps; her dolls and picture books; turn my study into a nursery."

When the Lafayette Square Opera House was erected next door, neighbors felt their sanctuary had been invaded. The Camerons stayed for two more years, before feeling "compelled to move, when living next door to a theater became intolerable."

10 Site of Lafayette Square Opera House (now the Howard T. Markey National Courts Building)

A theater was built in 1895 on the site of the 1830s Rodgers House, which was razed in 1894. Designed by the Chicago firm of Wood & Lovell, the opera house overlooked Lafayette Square and was built for Uriah H. Painter.

The six-story building had a soaring facade, with Ionic columns framing the main entrance on Madison

Buildings on the east side of Lafayette Square, 1916. *From left to right:* partial view of the Cosmos Club (which also housed the National Geographic Society, with a separate entrance, beginning in 1891); the Robert G. Ingersoll House at 23 Madison Place; the Tayloe House at 21 Madison Place, home to Senator J. Donald Cameron and his wife, Elizabeth, from 1887 to 1897; and the Lafayette Square Opera House (later renamed the Belasco Theater). The U.S. Treasury Building can be seen in the distance.

Place, as well as below the huge cornice. The beige brickwork was decorated with three panels over triple arched windows placed over the main entry. The auditorium, which could seat about 1,800, was a blend of Beaux Arts, neoclassical, and Italian Renaissance styles, complete with lavishly ornate gilded plasterwork, three balconies, thirty boxes, and a graceful but towering proscenium arch, again, coated with gilded plaster decorations.

Along with the National Theater, the grandiose Lafayette Square Opera House was the main venue for opera, plays, and ballet at the turn of the twentieth century in Washington. Among those who performed on its stage were Enrico Caruso, Sarah Bernhardt, and Ethel Barrymore.

In 1906, the opera house was taken over by the Shuberts and David Belasco and was renamed the Belasco Theater. By the early years of the Depression, the Shuberts gave up the Belasco, and by 1935, it was converted to a movie house. During the late 1930s, legitimate theater made a short-lived and not very successful return, but in 1940, the Belasco and nearby properties, including the Tayloe House and Cosmos Club, were acquired by the federal government, which used the Belasco for a warehouse and offices (all of the seats were removed from the theater at this time).

After America's entry into World War II, the Belasco was reopened as a Stage Door Canteen for the entertainment of servicemen. It closed at the start of 1946. During the Korean War, the Belasco was reopened as the Lafayette Square Club, again as a venue for entertaining servicemen.

In the early 1960s, with the reconstruction of Lafayette Square, many of the Belasco's neighbors were razed, until finally, in 1964, the Belasco itself was torn down to make way for the new Howard T. Markey National Courts Building.

→ **Turn right onto Pennsylvania Avenue, walking west along the pedestrian-only street.**

11 The White House

As the great-grandson of the second U.S. president, John Adams, and the grandson of the sixth, John Quincy Adams, Henry Adams was part of one of the country's greatest political dynasties.

When he first came to DC on a visit at age twelve, his father brought him to meet President Zachary Taylor. The young boy was not awed. As he wrote in *The Education of Henry Adams:* "As for the White House, all the boy's family had lived there, and, barring the eight years of Andrew Jackson's reign, had been more or less at home there ever since it was built. The boy thought he owned it, and took for granted that he should some day live in it."

Once he moved to DC, Adams always lived in close proximity to the White House. His residence coincided with ten presidential administrations (from Rutherford Hayes through Woodrow Wilson), and he was the intimate of several presidents and cabinet officers. He considered himself a behind-the-scenes advisor and confidante, calling himself a "stable-companion to statesmen," influencing most strongly the Hayes, Cleveland, McKinley, and Roosevelt administrations.

12 Eisenhower Executive Office Building

Seventeenth Street and Pennsylvania Avenue NW

From 1877 to 1880, Adams was given space to work here, under the auspices of the State Department. The building was then known as the State, War, and Navy Building.

Ernest Samuels, in his biography *Henry Adams* (1964), says Adams was assigned

a private desk with space for his personal copyist and . . . free access to the restricted archives. From the library windows there was a fine view across the Ellipse. Directly south were two small lagoons adjoining the vaguely edged tidal swamplands. The report of a fowling piece occasionally startled the reflections of statesmen—and historians, for the low ground was still favored by duck hunters. The great South Front, which had been completed in 1875, presented to an awed nation the most extensive and colossal version of a French chateau yet seen on the continent, a baroque kaleidoscope of pavilions, porticoes, porches, colonnades, and chimneys, topped with a mansard roof, the effect French neoclassical or Italian Renaissance, depending on the tourist's mood.

This was also the office of John Hay when he worked for the State Department and served as secretary of state.

13 Renwick Gallery

Pennsylvania Avenue NW at Seventeenth Street

William Corcoran, the Adamses' early landlord, was a serious art collector and a neighbor on Lafayette Square. When his collection became too large to accommodate in his home, he commissioned this building in 1858. The gallery was nearly completed when the Civil War began, and it was commandeered by the Union army for use by the Quartermaster Corps. In 1870, the gallery was incorporated as a nonprofit institution and finally opened to the public in 1871. Henry Adams, with his own interest in art, would have visited.

The collection was most famous for a marble sculpture of a nude white woman in manacles by Hiram Powers called *The Greek Slave* (now in the collection of the Smithsonian American Art Museum). It was so controversial that the museum arranged separate visiting hours for men and women. Children under sixteen were not allowed.

➜ **Turn right onto Seventeenth Street, and walk north one block.**

14 Metropolitan Club

SW corner of Seventeenth and H Streets NW

The Metropolitan Club was chartered in 1872. Members built a permanent clubhouse on the southwest corner of Seventeenth and H Streets NW in 1883. When that building was damaged by fire in 1904, they built a new Renaissance Revival building, completed in 1908 and still standing.

Members included some of the most important men of the day: congressmen, cabinet officials, Supreme Court justices, bankers, businessmen, American and foreign diplomats, military men, literary men, journalists, scientists, and professionals in law and medicine. Henry Adams and John Hay were members, as were the banker and philanthropist William Corcoran, banker George Riggs, Lincoln's postmaster general Montgomery Blair, Admiral Charles Wilkes, General William T. Sherman, personal secretary to Lincoln John Nicolay, DC governor Alexander "Boss" Shepherd, and Senator Charles Sumner.

➜ **Walk west on H Street two blocks, then bear right onto Pennsylvania Avenue and walk one more block. Walk around the small triangular park to the I Street side.**

15 Arts Club of Washington

2017 I Street NW

The only house Adams lived in that remains standing in DC has been preserved by the Arts Club of Washington, a private club that houses public art galleries. If you take this tour on Tuesday through Saturday during their regular business hours, you can ring the bell and ask to be admitted to the galleries.

The Arts Club has also preserved a second house next door and combined the two (creating strange half staircases throughout the inside, since the other house is on a higher foundation). Additions have also been made at the rear (where the Adams family would have had their cook house, wash house, and stable). But you can see the front reception room and dining room on the first floor, and the formal parlor on the second.

Adams lived here with his parents during the winter of 1860–61. Aware that he was witnessing a historic time, he kept a journal, wrote dispatches for a Boston newspaper, and later published an essay, "The Great Secession Winter," which the historian Garry Wills describes as "full of inside information" and still "repeatedly cited in treatments of the Civil War's onset."

Adams wrote that treason was in the air:

Ten years had passed since his last visit, but very little had changed. . . . [T]he same rude colony was camped in the same forest, with the same unfinished Greek temples for work-rooms, and sloughs for roads. The government had an air of social instability and incompleteness that went far to support the right of secession in theory as in fact; but right or wrong, secession was likely to be easy where there was so little to secede from. The Union was a sentiment, but not much more, and in December 1860, the sentiment about the Capitol was chiefly hostile, so far as it made itself felt.

→ **Take I Street east three blocks, to Farragut Square. Go around the square to the northern side and enter the Farragut North Metro Station. Take a Red Line train toward Glenmont. Go two station stops, to Gallery Place, then change to a Green or Yellow Line train toward Greenbelt. Go five stops to the Georgia Avenue/ Petworth station, then exit on the northbound side. Cross New Hampshire Avenue and turn left onto Rock Creek Church Road. After a ten-minute walk, on a gentle uphill slope, passing the Soldier's Home grounds on your right, Rock Creek Church Road intersects with Webster Street NW. (Alternately, you can take a short ride on the H8 bus.) You will see the cemetery entrance on the left. The Adams gravesite is located in Section E. If you are facing the front of St. Paul's Church, inside the cemetery, that section will be on your right. The grave is in the middle of Section E; look for a wall of tall bushes. Alternately, you can request a map of the 86-acre cemetery, available at the cemetery office.**

16 Rock Creek Church Cemetery

Rock Creek Church Road at Webster Street NW

Adams commissioned another friend, the sculptor Augustus Saint-Gaudens, to create a memorial for his wife, Clover. Saint-Gaudens was the foremost American sculptor of the second half of the nineteenth century. He created the Shaw Monument on the Boston Common and the Sherman Statue in Central Park, among other notable works.

Adams asked that Saint-Gaudens create a figure that symbolized, like the Japanese figure Kwannon, "the acceptance, intellectually of the inevitable." He noted

Adams Memorial, Rock Creek Church Cemetery

that he did not wish to see the work until it was finished, instructing Saint-Gaudens to direct any questions about its execution to their common friend, the painter John La Farge. Adams wrote in 1891:

At times I begin to doubt whether Saint-Gaudens will ever let the work be finished. I half suspect that my refusal, to take the responsibility of formally approving the clay, frightened him. Had I cared less about it, I should have gone to see it, as he wished, and should have admired it as much as he liked, but I had many misgivings that I should not be wholly satisfied with his rendering of the idea; and that I might not be able to conceal my disappointment. . . . I knew well that I should only injure Saint-Gaudens's work without obtaining my own ideal by suggesting changes, for the artist is usually right in regarding changes, not his own, as blemishes. From the first I told Saint-Gaudens that he should be absolutely free from interference.

John Hay saw the finished sculpture before Adams and reported in a letter:

The work is indescribably noble and imposing. It is to my mind Saint-Gaudens's master-piece. It is full of poetry and suggestion, infinite wisdom, a past without beginning and a future without end, a repose after limitless experience, a peace to which nothing matters—all are embodied in this austere and beautiful face and form.

The memorial is set in an outdoor room, or open-air chapel, defined by the raised octagonal pebble floor, the granite bench forming one side (designed by noted architect Sanford White), and the boxwood hedges surrounding the whole. The bronze figure sits on a granite rock imported from Quincy, Massachusetts. As Cynthia Mills writes in *Beyond Grief: Sculpture and Wonder in the Gilded Age Cemetery* (2014), the scandalous circumstances of Clover's suicide and Henry's innate sense of privacy drove him to seek "a newer conception of consolation" than most sentimental funerary art of the time, something that "synthesized Western and Eastern tastes, the rational and nonrational, and ultimately male and female."

The memorial became a favorite retreat for Adams, and he visited often, finding comfort in this contemplative spot. Adams was also interred at the gravesite, next to his wife. His will stipulated: "no inscription, dates, letters, or other attempt at memorial" should be placed at the grave. The memorial is arguably the most important piece of figurative art in all of Washington, DC.

Portraits

Mark Twain

November 30, 1835–April 21, 1910

There is something good and motherly about Washington, the grand old benevolent National Asylum for the Helpless.

Samuel Langhorne Clemens, who wrote under the pen name Mark Twain, is the author of fourteen novels, including *The Adventures of Tom Sawyer* (1876) and *The Adventures of Huckleberry Finn* (1885). He also published ten collections of short fiction, essays, a play, and travelogues and memoirs.

Twain lived in DC in 1867, working briefly as a secretary for Senator William Morris Stewart of Nevada. He lived in a boardinghouse at the northwest corner of Fourteenth and F Streets NW, run by Virginia Wells. According to Senator Stewart, who also lived at this address, he terrorized his landlady: "He would lurch around the halls, pretending to be intoxicated. . . . He would burn the light in his bedroom all night. . . . Pretty soon he took to smoking cigars in bed" and ruined her sheets with burn holes.

Another journalist, Hiram J. Ramsdell, wrote of this boardinghouse where he also lived briefly, in an 1883 article in the *San Francisco Bulletin*. Several journalists took rooms there, including George Alfred Townsend and Jerome B. Stillson. Ramsdell describes Twain's room as the smallest in the house, "a little back room, with a sheet-iron stove, a dirty, musty carpet of the cheapest description, a bed and two or three common chairs."

Mark Twain

Ramsdell continues: "At that time we all did our work in our rooms, and when one of us got tired we went to the room of one of the others. If the other fellow was working hard he snubbed the visitor, if he was idling he welcomed him. At Twain's room, however, the visitor was always welcomed, for by nature Twain is so lazy that he will not work if there is an excuse for loafing."

He wrote that the back room was "a novelty, a museum, a hermit's cave, a den for a wild animal, and the wild animal was there. . . . I wish you could see it today, in the light of Mark Twain's present reputation and his half million of money. I am rather hardened now, but I remember it shocked me at the time" because "the bed seemed to be unmade for a week, the slops had not been carried out for a fortnight, the room was sour with tobacco-smoke, the floor, dirty enough to begin with, was littered with newspapers." He concludes that he never imagined Twain or his writing "would amount to anything, and probably, he did not think it would either."

Twain finished the manuscript of his book *The Innocents Abroad* while in DC. That book, published in 1869, chronicles his travels in the Holy Land. His experiences in DC inspired his next novel, *The Gilded Age* (1873), a satire of the city's political and social life, cowritten with Charles Dudley Warner. His label for the post–Civil War period has stuck: it describes the economic growth, widening divide between the rich and poor, and political corruption that are hallmarks of the era.

Some quotes from the novel give a good sense of the whole:

You stand at the back of the capitol to treat yourself to a view, and it is a very noble one. You understand, the capitol stands upon the verge of a high piece of table land, a fine commanding position, and its front looks out over this noble situation for a city—but it don't see it, for the reason that when the capitol extension was decided upon, the property owners at once advanced their prices to such inhuman figures that the people went down and built their city in the muddy low marsh *behind* the temple of liberty; so now the lordly front of the building, with its imposing colonnades, its projecting, graceful wings, its picturesque groups of statuary, and its long terraced ranges of steps, flowing down in white marble waves to the ground, merely looks out upon a sorrowful little desert of cheap boarding houses. . . .

Now you wrench your gaze loose and you look down in front of you and see the broad Pennsylvania Avenue stretching straight ahead for a mile or more till it brings up against the iron fence in front of a pillared granite pile, the Treasury building—an edifice that would command respect in any capital. The stores and hotels that wall in this broad avenue are mean, and cheap, and dingy, and are better left without comment. Beyond the Treasury is a fine large white barn, with wide unhandsome grounds about it. The President lives there. It is ugly enough outside, but that is nothing to what it is inside. Dreariness, flimsiness, bad taste reduced to mathematical completeness is what the inside offers to the eye. . . .

It seemed to him a feverish, unhealthy atmosphere in which lunacy would be easily developed. He fancied that everybody attached to himself an exaggerated importance. . . . People were introduced to each other as from this or that state, not from cities or towns, and this gave a largeness to their representative feeling. All the women talked politics as naturally and glibly as they talk fashion or literature elsewhere. There was always some exciting topic at the Capitol, or some huge slander was rising up like a miasmatic exhalation from the Potomac.

Ambrose Bierce

June 24, 1842–Unknown

Journalist, poet, short story writer, and satirist, Ambrose Bierce lived in DC from 1899 through 1913. While in Washington, Bierce completed his *Devil's Dictionary* (1911) and his word-usage compendium *Write It Right* (1909).

Bierce served in the Union army during the Civil War, then began his career as a journalist. Although usually associated with San Francisco, Bierce lived in DC for the last fifteen years of his known life. According

Ambrose Bierce

to M. A. Schaffner, in his essay "A Good Opinion of Bierce" (2008):

He was first sent here by William Randolph Hearst to lead the *Examiner*'s fight against a "funding bill" pushed by the railroad baron Collis P. Huntington. Huntington's Southern Pacific Railroad had been the beneficiary of substantial government loans and land grants—many of them provided as Bierce and his comrades were under fire. The "funding bill" would provide a 99 year extension to the deadline for repayment of $75,000,000. But Hearst had chosen his agent well. Bierce's reportage sold very well but was anything but objective. A mild sample would be this statement from his account of Huntington's first day of testimony on the Hill: "Today he not only appeared, but took his hand out of all manner of pockets long enough to hold it up and be sworn."

The bill was defeated, but Bierce remained.

Bierce is perhaps best remembered for his short story "An Occurrence at Owl Creek Bridge" (1890). He published twelve books during his lifetime, a combination of essays, fiction, poetry, and nonfiction. In October 1913, he left DC for a tour of his old Civil War battlefields, then traveled to Mexico to observe Pancho Villa's army during the Mexican Revolution. He was never heard from or seen again.

Homes he rented in DC still stand and can be found at: 1368 Euclid Street NW (the Olympia Apartments); 18 Logan Circle NW; 1825 Nineteenth Street NW; and 1321 Fairmont Street NW (El Dorado Apartments). In a private letter to a friend dated June 14, 1904, Bierce wrote: "The most *contented* years of my life lately were the two or three that I passed here before Washington folk found out that I was an author. The fact has leaked out, and although not a soul of them buys and reads my books some of them bore me insupportably with their ignorant compliments and unwelcome attentions."

In *The Devil's Dictionary,* he defined a "Washingtonian" as "A Potomac tribesman who exchanged the privilege of governing himself for the advantage of good government. In justice to him it should be said that he did not want to."

A poem by Ambrose Bierce:

A YEAR'S CASUALTIES

Slain as they lay by the secret, slow,
Pitiless hand of an unseen foe,

Two score thousand old soldiers have crossed
The river to join the loved and lost.
In the space of a year their spirits fled,
Silent and white, to the camp of the dead.

One after one, they fall asleep
And the pension agents awake to weep,
And orphaned statesmen are loud in their wail
As the souls flit by on the evening gale.
O Father of Battles, pray give us release
From the horrors of peace, the horrors of peace!

Elinor Wylie

September 7, 1885–December 16, 1928

Elinor Wylie is the author of five books of poems, including *Nets to the Catch the Wind* (1921) and *Angels and Earthly Creatures* (1928), and four novels, including *Jennifer Lorn* (1923) and *The Orphan Angel* (1926). Her *Collected Poems* (1932) and *Collected Prose* (1933) were published posthumously.

Wylie was born into a socially prominent family, and she scandalized the society world with her multiple marriages and affairs. Her first husband, Philip Simmons Hichborn, was mentally unstable and abusive. Wylie had one son with him, but she abandoned both husband and son to live with another married man, Horace Wiley, a DC lawyer. When her affair was widely reported in newspapers, she was ostracized by her family, and the couple moved to England and lived under an assumed name. Wylie's first husband committed suicide, and Horace attained a divorce, so Wylie and Horace returned to the United States and married. Wylie's third husband was the poet and editor William Rose Benét, but this marriage, too, was short-lived.

Wylie became part of the literary community centered around Greenwich Village in New York. She worked as poetry editor for *Vanity Fair* (1923–25) and a contributing editor of the *New Republic* (1926–28).

Two of her DC houses still stand. The first, at 1707 N Street NW, is where Wylie lived with her first husband, from 1906 to 1910. A second address at 2153 Florida Avenue NW is the location where Wylie lived briefly (from 1920 to 1921) after separating from her second husband.

A poem by Elinor Wylie:

WILD PEACHES

1

When the world turns completely upside down
You say we'll emigrate to the Eastern Shore
Aboard a river-boat from Baltimore;
We'll live among wild peach trees, miles from town,
You'll wear a coonskin cap, and I a gown
Homespun, dyed butternut's dark gold colour.
Lost, like your lotus-eating ancestor,
We'll swim in milk and honey till we drown.
The winter will be short, the summer long,
The autumn amber-hued, sunny and hot,
Tasting of cider and of scuppernong;
All seasons sweet, but autumn best of all.
The squirrels in their silver fur will fall
Like falling leaves, like fruit, before your shot.

2

The autumn frosts will lie upon the grass
Like bloom on grapes of purple-brown and gold.
The misted early mornings will be cold;
The little puddles will be roofed with glass.
The sun, which burns from copper into brass,

Melts these at noon, and makes the boys unfold
Their knitted mufflers; full as they can hold
Fat pockets dribble chestnuts as they pass.
Peaches grow wild, and pigs can live in clover;
A barrel of salted herrings lasts a year;
The spring begins before the winter's over.
By February you may find the skins
Of garter snakes and water moccasins
Dwindled and harsh, dead-white and cloudy-clear.

3

When April pours the colors of a shell
Upon the hills, when every little creek
Is shot with silver from the Chesapeake
In shoals new-minted by the ocean swell,
When strawberries go begging, and the sleek
Blue plums lie open to the blackbird's beak,
We shall live well—we shall live very well.
The months between the cherries and the peaches
Are brimming cornucopias which spill
Fruits red and purple, sombre-bloomed and black;
Then, down rich fields and frosty river beaches
We'll trample bright persimmons, while you kill
Bronze partridge, speckled quail, and canvasback.

4

Down to the Puritan marrow of my bones
There's something in this richness that I hate.
I love the look, austere, immaculate,
Of landscapes drawn in pearly monotones.
There's something in my very blood that owns
Bare hills, cold silver on a sky of slate,
A thread of water, churned to milky spate
Streaming through slanted pastures fenced with stones.
I love those skies, thin blue or snowy gray,
Those fields sparse-planted, rendering meagre sheaves;

That spring, briefer than apple-blossom's breath,
Summer, so much too beautiful to stay,
Swift autumn, like a bonfire of leaves,
And sleepy winter, like the sleep of death.

The Jazz Age, 1920–1930

Langston Hughes

Langston Hughes and the Harlem Renaissance along U Street

Despite being named for a neighborhood in New York City, the arts movement known as the Harlem Renaissance was centered in several cities. DC was one of the most significant hubs of what was known at the time as the New Negro Movement; one could even claim that Washington is where the movement was born. This walking tour focuses on the U Street neighborhood, where several prominent writers, musicians, and artists lived in close proximity.

In the 1920s, Washington could boast of an impressive a number of institutions that served and hired African Americans, notably Howard University, the premier African American university (which Zora Neale Hurston called "the capstone of Negro education in the world"); the federal government, which hired African Americans for a variety of jobs considered both well-paying and prestigious; the Association for the Study of Negro Life and History; and the M Street High School (now Paul Laurence Dunbar High), the top African American high school in the United States. DC had the largest and most established population of middle-class African Americans from the turn of the century through the 1930s. Unlike in New York, most properties in the segregated neighborhoods in the

Langston Hughes and the Harlem Renaissance along U Street

W ST NW

1) Lincoln Theater
2) Ben's Chili Bowl,
   formerly the
   Minnehaha Theater
3) Ben's Next Door,
   formerly the Music Box
   and the Jungle Inn
4) Starbucks Coffee,
   formerly Pendleton's
   High Grade Book and
   Job Printing

1 2 3

FLORIDA AVE NW

10TH ST NW

V ST NW

Garnet-
Patterson
Junior High
School
21

13TH ST NW

"Black
Broadway"
23

Former
Washington
Eagle Office

U ST NW

4 **25**
M Metro
Plaza

24
True
Reformer's
Hall

22
Prince Hall
Masonic Temple

M
U STREET

19 **20**
Former
Murray's
Palace
Casino

STREET

Madame Lillian
Evanti House
17

18
Grimké
School

Richard
Bruce
Nugent
House
13

12TH ST NW

T Street
Pool Halls
16

T ST NW

12

14
Addison
Scurlock
House site

VERMONT AVE NW

Whitelaw
apartments

15
Thurgood
Marshall
Center for
Service and
Heritage,
former 12th
Street YMCA

WESTMINSTER
ST NW

Jessie Redmon
Fauset House

10TH ST NW

10

Duke
lington
ouses

S ST NW

VERMONT AVE NW

11TH ST NW

FRENCH ST NW

middle of the city (Shaw, Cardozo, LeDroit Park, and Pleasant Plains) were actually owned by African Americans. Property was more affordable in DC than New York, both to own and to rent, making a middle-class lifestyle more attainable there.

The Harlem Renaissance arguably began with the 1925 publication of *The New Negro,* an anthology edited by the DC resident Alain Locke. A Harvard graduate and the first black recipient of a Rhodes Scholarship, Locke was the chair of the Philosophy Department at Howard and also the faculty advisor for the university's literary society and magazine.

→ **Start in front of 1250 U Street NW, on the U Street Metro Plaza by the DC Department of Parks and Recreation Office and the SunTrust Bank. Look across the street at the three buildings facing you.**

1 Lincoln Theater

1215 U Street NW

The only remaining of three major movie palaces on U Street, the Lincoln Theater opened in 1922 under African American management. With 1,600 seats, the Lincoln was a classy, first-run movie house during a time when such establishments were strictly segregated. If you went to the movies here, you dressed up! The Lincoln has been restored and is now used as a performance hall. This was also the site of the Lincoln Colonnade, a popular club entered through the alleyway that was in the basement level of the theater.

Lincoln Theater

2 The Minnehaha Theater (now Ben's Chili Bowl)

1213 U Street NW

You can still see the outlines of the original arched entry to the Minnehaha Theater peeking from behind the modern restaurant signs. Nickelodeon theaters were small storefront operations that showed silent films, typically fifteen to twenty minutes long, with live piano or organ accompaniment. Admission was five cents. This theater was built in 1910 and is one of the best-preserved nickelodeon buildings still standing in the United States. The Minnehaha operated until 1920. A pool hall later replaced the theater, and in 1958, the building was purchased by Virginia and Ben Ali. Ben's Chili Bowl remains one of the oldest continuous businesses in the neighborhood, a much-beloved institution known for its famous chili half-smokes.

3 Site of the Music Box and the Jungle Inn (now Ben's Next Door)

1212 U Street NW

From 1935 to 1938, this was a club managed by Ferdinand Joseph LaMothe, aka "Jelly Roll" Morton. After he was stabbed multiple times in the head and chest by a disgruntled customer, Morton's wife, Mabel, insisted that he leave the business (and some argue this attack helped lead to his early demise). Although Morton's residency in DC was brief, it was while here that he was recorded by the folklorist Alan Lomax, who made more than eight hours of recordings of the interviews and music that helped to secure Morton's fame. (Later released on CDs, the recordings earned two Grammy awards.) Morton is known for developments in ragtime and stride piano styles; he is considered the first serious jazz composer.

→ **Walk a half block west to the corner of U and Thirteenth Streets.**

4 Site of Robert L. Pendleton's High Grade Book and Job Printing (now Starbucks Coffee)

1216 U Street NW

From 1922 to 1923, this was the rented headquarters of the Association for the Study of Negro Life and History, founded by Dr. Carter G. Woodson. Although the Association later moved to its permanent headquarters at 1538 Ninth Street NW, it had its first home in this location, thanks to the generosity of Robert Pendleton, an African American business owner and early supporter of the Association. Woodson, the man who inaugurated Negro History Week (now expanded to Black History Month), was a major figure in the collection and preservation of African American history. He briefly hired Langston Hughes as a clerk, and a monetary grant from the Association supported the anthropological research of Zora Neale Hurston, resulting in her book *Mules and Men* (1935).

Woodson was born to former slaves in Virginia, and although he attended school only sporadically as a child because his family needed his help on their farm, he eventually became the second trained black historian in the United States (after W. E. B. Du Bois) when he earned a PhD from Harvard University at the age of thirty-seven.

He founded the Association for the Study of Negro Life and History in 1915. The mission of the organization, according to Woodson, was "the collection of sociological and historical data on the Negro, the study of peoples of African blood, the publishing of books in the field, and the promotion of harmony between the races by acquainting the one with the other."

The Association published books, issued reports, gave grants to young scholars, and published the *Journal of Negro History,* the first scholarly journal in the field. Most of the funding for the Association came from Dr. Woodson himself. Woodson taught in DC at both of the public high schools for African Americans, the M Street High School (now Dunbar High), and Armstrong Manual Training School (where he was principal). He later became dean of the School of Liberal Arts at Howard University.

➤ **Continue west on U Street.**

5 Site of Jean Toomer's Residence (now The Ellington)

1351 U Street NW

Jean Toomer lived here with his grandfather, P. B. S. Pinchback, the first African American state governor (he was governor of Louisiana from 1872 to 1873). Pinchback purchased the house on this site in 1893 and served as a U.S. marshal. He entertained lavishly as a member of the black elite. Toomer was living here in 1923 when his book *Cane* was published, one of the earliest masterpieces of the Harlem Renaissance, and its publication electrified other young writers. *Cane* is a mixture of prose sketches and poems, many set among the restaurants, pool halls, and churches located in the nearby working-class Seventh Street district.

Toomer and Langston Hughes were friends, and they shared a fascination with Seventh Street (the section between Florida Avenue and M Street), which inspired a number of Hughes's poems—including most from his second book of poems, *Fine Clothes to the Jew* (1927). (The title of that book comes from the used-clothing business, then known as the "rag trade" and dominated by Jewish merchants. Clothing was the last thing someone in straightened circumstances might sell.)

Not only was Washington at the time segregated by race, but the African American community was segregated too, divided by skin color and class. Hughes wrote in *The Big Sea* (1940):

Seventh Street was a sweet relief. Seventh Street is the long, old, dirty street, where the ordinary Negroes hang out, folks with practically no family tree at all, folks who draw no color line between mulattoes and deep dark-browns, folks who work hard for a living with their hands. On Seventh Street in 1924 they played the blues, ate watermelon, barbecue, and fish sandwiches, shot pool, told tall tales, looked at the dome of the Capitol and laughed out loud. . . . I tried to write poems like the songs they sang on Seventh Street—gay songs, because you had to be gay or die; sad songs, because you couldn't help being sad sometimes. But gay or sad, you kept on living and you kept on going. Their songs—those of Seventh Street— had the pulse beat of the people who keep on going. . . . I liked the barrel houses of Seventh Street, the shouting churches, and the songs.

According to *The Guide to Black Washington* (1999), by Sandra Fitzpatrick and Maria R. Goodwin, "Seventh Street was as vital and bustling as its neighbor, U Street, but in a seamier, louder way." It was populated largely by "southern rural immigrants who flocked to the north for jobs during World War I and during the Depression. Noise and music from the traffic, poolrooms, storefront churches, barbershops, liquor stores, flophouses, and lunch counters mingled together."

In *Cane* (1923), Jean Toomer wrote:

Seventh Street is a bastard of Prohibition and the War. A crude-boned, soft-skinned wedge . . . breathing its loafer air, jazz songs and love, thrusting unconscious rhythms, black-reddish blood into the white and whitewashed wood of Washington. Stale soggy wood of Washington. . . . White and whitewash disappear in blood. Who set you flowing? Flowing down the smooth asphalt of Seventh Street, in shanties, in brick office buildings, theaters, drug stores, restaurants, and cabarets? Eddying on the corners? Swirling like a blood-red smoke up where the buzzards fly in heaven? God would not dare to suck black red blood. . . .

He would duck his head in shame and call for the Judgment Day. Who set you flowing?

6 The *Washington Sentinel* newspaper (now the Hamiltonian Gallery)

1353 U Street NW

This building was constructed for one of several African American newspapers in DC, when the press was segregated. Note the printing-press design in brick at the top of the building's facade. Langston Hughes worked here for a few months.

Throughout his youth, Hughes was torn by issues of class. Members of his mother's family were descendants of one of the most prominent African Americans of the nineteenth century, John Mercer Langston, who was the first African American theological college graduate in the United States, the first African American elected to public office (township clerk of Brownhelm, Ohio), dean of Howard University Law School, U.S. minister to Haiti, and U.S. congressman (representing Petersburg, Virginia). Hughes was Langston's greatnephew. On Hughes's father's side, however, he was firmly working class, and Hughes increasingly felt a commitment to capturing the lives of the working-class African American majority in his poetry.

When Hughes first arrived in DC, he lived with his Langston cousins, who encouraged him to seek prestigious employment as a congressional page or journalist. Hughes worked at this location only briefly, because he disliked selling advertisements, which was his main job duty. After leaving the newspaper, he took a very unprestigious job, which led to a split with his cousins, at a wet-wash laundry.

→ **Walk to the corner of Fourteenth Street and turn left. Walk two blocks south of Fourteenth.**

7 Club Bali (now Matchbox Restaurant)

1901 Fourteenth Street NW

Built in 1907 as a billiards hall and bowling alley, this building has seen multiple uses, including a Chevrolet showroom, a restaurant, and a bar called Wiseman's Lounge. Its most important historical uses were as an exhibition hall in 1937 for the "National Memorial to the Progress of the Negro Race in America," and as one of the city's premier jazz clubs from 1940 to 1954, Club Bali. Club Bali hosted such acts as Louis Armstrong, Billie Holiday, and Charlie Ventura. The club closed after its colorful owner, Bennie Caldwell, was convicted of jury tampering. Arena Stage bought the building in 1984, prior to the neighborhood's resurgence, and helped the area reclaim its identity as an arts district. In 2012, the building was purchased by the current restaurant owners.

→ **Continue south to S Street, then turn right and walk two blocks to the corner of S and Fifteenth Streets NW.**

8 "Half-Way House," Georgia Douglas Johnson Residence

1461 S Street NW (marked with a historic plaque)

Home of the Saturday Nighters Club, a literary salon, this house is one of the most important extant sites of the Harlem Renaissance period. Gathering weekly for cake, wine, and stimulating discussions, the salon

"Half-Way House," home of Georgia Douglas Johnson and meeting place of the Saturday Nighters Club

brought together the era's young, ambitious writers as well as older mentors. Regular attendees included Kelly Miller, dean of Howard University; his daughter, the playwright May Miller; critic and anthologist Alain Locke; historian Carter G. Woodson; Angelina Weld Grimké, the author of the first play by an African American to receive a fully staged, professional production; writer and actor Richard Bruce Nugent; essayist and playwright Marita Bonner; poet and short-story writer Alice Dunbar-Nelson; poet and musician William Waring Cuney; novelist Jessie Redmon Fauset; Langston Hughes; Jean Toomer; and Zora Neale Hurston.

In *The Big Sea* (1940), Langston Hughes described Johnson as "a charming woman poet" who "turned her house into a salon for us" where writers could "eat Mrs. Johnson's cake and drink her wine and talk poetry and books and plays." In a private letter, novelist Jessie Fauset wrote: "She is so kind and charming and stimulating. I covet her disposition."

Johnson moved to DC with her husband (a lawyer) and two sons in 1909 or 1910. In 1912, her husband was appointed by President William Howard Taft to the prestigious position of recorder of deeds for the District of Columbia. Despite the demands of motherhood and wifedom, and with little support from her husband (who urged on her the traditional homemaker role), Douglas Johnson was able to carve out time to write. In the early 1920s, Jean Toomer approached her about hosting "weekly conversations among writers here in Washington." Toomer thought that others, like him, might be feeling starved for intellectual company. Hosting these weekly Saturday-night gatherings was a role that Douglas Johnson relished, as the evenings undoubtedly not only allowed her to showcase her gracious hospitality but also served to enhance her standing among the writers of the time.

In 1925, her husband of nearly twenty-two years died, leaving Douglas Johnson to provide for herself and two teenaged sons. Through fierce will and hard work, she put Peter through college at Dartmouth and medical school at Howard University, and she put Henry Lincoln Jr. through Bowdoin College and law school at Howard. She did substitute teaching, worked as a clerk, and did some hack writing work until she was finally able to secure a more stable and financially rewarding job as the commissioner of conciliation in the Department of Labor in 1925. Douglas Johnson also published a syndicated newspaper column from 1926 to 1932, managed a letter-writing club, and wrote short stories. Georgia Douglas Johnson was the author of four books of poems, six plays, and thirty-two song lyrics, making her one of the best-published women authors of the Harlem Renaissance. She died in her home in 1966.

→ **Retrace your steps east on S Street to the corner of Fourteenth. Cross Fourteenth Street.**

9 Site of the Washington City Orphan Asylum

Southeast corner of Fourteenth and S Streets NW

The first significant building in this neighborhood stood on this corner. It was built shortly after a horse-drawn streetcar line began running on Fourteenth Street. The Orphan Asylum, a large building in the Italianate Villa style, was built in 1865 and 1866 and stood for almost one hundred years, until it was demolished in 1963.

→ **Continue east on S Street for one more block. Turn right on Thirteenth Street. The first stop will be on the right side of the street.**

10 Homes of the teenage Duke Ellington

1805 Thirteenth Street NW (marked with a historic plaque)

Duke Ellington lived in seven addresses in DC; two are on this block. Ellington lived in this house with his family beginning in 1910, and in another farther down the block, at 1816 Thirteenth Street NW, beginning in 1914. These are the locations where he lived in his teenage years, when he first became serious about music. He took piano lessons from a neighbor, Henry Grant, and began visiting area clubs (while still underage).

This street was a prominent residential street for middle-class African Americans through the first half of the 1900s, and neighbors included doctors, businessmen, and government clerks. Ellington's first gig with his own band, Duke's Serenaders, took place at the True Reformers Hall, on U Street, and his subsequent band, the Washingtonians, was one of the leading society bands in the city. Ellington moved to Harlem in 1923.

When the U.S. Mint issued a coin representing DC in 2009, Duke Ellington was portrayed on it, making him the first musician and the first African American to be featured on a U.S. circulating coin. He is remembered in the city with a high school and a bridge named in his honor.

→ **Continue walking north on Thirteenth Street.**

11 Home of Jessie Redmon Fauset

1812 Thirteenth Street NW

Fauset rented rooms here, one of five locations in the city where she rented while teaching at the M Street High School. M Street was such a prestigious public school that many families moved to the area just for the opportunity to send their children to the school whose students regularly outscored their white counterparts on standardized tests, and where most teachers had advanced degrees and were paid on a par with white teachers.

Fauset was the author of four novels, as well as poems, essays, and reviews. In addition to editing the *Crisis,* the official publication of the NAACP, she edited and was the primary writer for the *Brownies' Book,* a magazine for African American children.

At M Street High, she taught French and Latin from 1907 through 1919, after which she moved to New York to become literary editor of the *Crisis.* In that position, she mentored several younger writers, such as Claude McKay, Countee Cullen, Arna Bontemps, Nella Larsen, and Langston Hughes. In her prominent position, she influenced top African American leaders to support the important role the arts could play in what was then called "racial uplift." Fauset was a guiding spirit for the Harlem Renaissance and for the beginnings of literary modernism in general.

Hughes wrote: "Jessie Fauset at the *Crisis,* Charles Johnson at *Opportunity,* and Alain Locke in Washington, were the three people who midwifed the so-called New Negro Literature into being. Kind and critical—but not too critical for the young—they nursed us along until our books were born."

This is a good spot to remember another prominent teacher, Kelly Miller. Miller was a major figure during Reconstruction, and his widespread influence helped to make the Harlem Renaissance and the civil rights eras possible. Professor and administrator at Howard University for more than forty years, Miller served as a math professor (1890), a sociology professor (1895–1934), and dean of the College of Arts and Sciences (1907–19). He wrote a syndicated column that was published in more than one hundred African American newspapers. His most prominent book, *Race*

Adjustment (1908), was a crucial early text challenging racist notions of black inferiority.

In an essay in *Opportunity Magazine* published in 1928, he wrote:

The Washington Negro has the only complete school system in the country practically under his own control. . . . The colored high and normal schools enroll over three thousand pupils above the eighth grade level. This number of secondary students cannot be approximated in any other city—not even New York, Philadelphia and Chicago, with a much larger total Negro population. . . . The Negroes of Washington have reached the point of complete professional self sufficiency. Howard has turned out an army of physicians, lawyers, teachers and clergymen. . . . The capital furnishes the best opportunity and facilities for the expression of the Negro's innate gayety of soul. Washington is still the Negro's Heaven, and it will be many a moon before Harlem will be able to take away her scepter.

Miller was born less than a year after the Emancipation Proclamation, narrowly escaping slavery. He described himself as one of the "first fruits of the Civil War, one of the first African Americans who learned to read, write and cipher in public schools." He was the first African American to attend Johns Hopkins University, where he studied advanced mathematics, physics, and astronomy. He was also Howard University's first professor of sociology, making crucial developments to the field. He is remembered as an inspiring teacher and excellent administrator.

Whitelaw Apartments, formerly the Whitelaw Hotel

12 Whitelaw Hotel (now Whitelaw Apartments)

1839 Thirteenth Street NW

Built in 1913, the Whitelaw was the city's only first-class hotel and apartment building for African American visitors and residents. Named for the African American financier John Whitelaw Lewis, it was designed by the African American architect Isaiah T. Hatton. Note the fancy Italianate exterior, with its opulent design details. Guests included boxer Joe Louis, scientist George Washington Carver, and entertainers Cab

Calloway, Louis Armstrong, and Earl "Fatha" Hines. It is now administered by Manna, a social service organization, as apartments for people with moderate incomes.

→ **Continue to the corner, and turn right on T Street.**

13 Richard Bruce Nugent House

1231 T Street NW

Richard Bruce Nugent lived here with his grandmother from 1924 to 1926. Nugent was the author of "Smoke, Lillies, and Jade," a short story published in *Fire!!* in 1926, widely considered the first published black gay fiction. Active in the Saturday Nighters Club, Nugent later moved to Harlem, where he was a close friend of Zora Neale Hurston, Wallace Thurman, and Langston Hughes. In addition to writing, Nugent was an actor and visual artist.

14 Site of Addison Scurlock House (now replaced by a new residence)

1202 T Street NW

During his sixty-four-year career, Addison N. Scurlock documented the people, institutions, and events of African American Washington, chronicling the world of the elite middle class. Scurlock was the official photographer for Howard University, among other institutions. Scurlock moved to DC with his family in 1900 at age seventeen; in 1911, he opened his famous photography studio at 900 U Street NW. Scurlock lived at a house at this address with his wife, Mamie (who was his business manager) and his two sons, Robert and George (who joined the business as photographers in the 1930s). His remarkable collection of photos is now owned by the Smithsonian Institution National Museum of American History.

→ **Continue to the corner of Twelfth Street. Turn right and walk one block.**

15 Twelfth Street YMCA (now Thurgood Marshall Center for Service and Heritage)

1816 Twelfth Street NW

Langston Hughes lived in three locations in DC. The first, in the home of his cousins in the LeDroit Park neighborhood, no longer stands (it is now the site of College Hall, a dormitory on the Howard University campus). His second, at 1749 S Street, where his mother rented two unheated rooms for Hughes and his little stepbrother Kit, still stands and is a private residence. This is his third residence, then known as the Twelfth Street Y. Hughes rented a room on the third or fourth floor.

The Y was designed by W. Sidney Pittman, the first registered African American architect (and son-in-law of Booker T. Washington), and financed in part by John D. Rockefeller. President Theodore Roosevelt laid the cornerstone in 1908, and the building was completed in 1912 with rooms for fifty-four single-occupancy residents. Dr. Charles Drew, who pioneered the preservation of blood plasma, was an active member of the Twelfth Street Y. Later, this building was the site of early meetings for civil rights legislation organized

Twelfth Street YMCA (now the Thurgood Marshall Center for Service and Heritage)

by Thurgood Marshall (who would become the first African American Supreme Court justice). If you take this tour on a weekday, ring the bell and ask to see the exhibits in the front lobby, and the re-created dorm room on the second floor.

→ **Retrace your steps, heading north on Twelfth Street, and turn right on T Street.**

16 T Street Pool Halls

Stretching between the loud and bustling Seventh Street neighborhood south of Howard University to the classier section of Greater U Street, T Street was renowned in the 1920s for its pool halls. Such establishments as the Silver Slipper, the Ideal, the Subway, and the Southern Aid Building Billiard Parlor all were located on T Street. None still exists.

Pool halls were some of the most significant community gathering places for African American men in the 1920s, along with barbershops. According to *The Guide to Black Washington* (1999), they ranged "from poorly lit holes-in-the-wall to swanky emporiums" and held "more significance than the newspaper, since events and matters of interest are discussed here that never reach the press."

➜ **Continue to Vermont Avenue, and turn left. Walk one block.**

17 Madame Lillian Evanti House

1910 Vermont Avenue NW

Madame Evanti, born Annie Lillian Evans in DC, was the first African American to sing grand opera professionally. Evanti trained at Howard University, completing a BA in music in 1917 and marrying one of her professors, Roy W. Tibbs. Her friend Jessie Fauset was the person who suggested she combine her two last names of Evans and Tibbs to create the exotic stage name of Madame Evanti.

From 1925 through the outbreak of World War II, Evanti performed in France with the Nice and Paris opera companies. On her return to the United States, she cofounded the National Negro Opera Company and was one of its most renowned stars.

Evanti, who spoke five languages fluently, translated the libretto of *La traviata* into English. Also a composer, Evanti wrote music to accompany poems by Georgia Douglas Johnson, including "Hail to Fair Washington," which they hoped would become the city's anthem. Among other noted appearances, Evanti performed at the White House in 1934 for President Franklin D. Roosevelt. In the 1940s and 1950s, she toured Latin America as a goodwill ambassador for the U.S. State Department.

Madame Evanti's grandson Thurlow Tibbs Jr. was a major art collector and art dealer, and this house was later the site of his gallery. Tibbs began collecting when Madame Evanti left him her own collection of paintings in her will. Building on that bequest, he amassed a treasury of paintings, sculptures, prints, photographs, and drawings by visual artists of African descent; he organized exhibits such as the influential *Surrealism and the Afro-American Artist* and *Six Washington Masters*. After his death, the Evans-Tibbs Collection (and Tibbs's archives) was bequeathed to the Corcoran Gallery of Art. In 2015, the Evans-Tibbs Collection was acquired by the National Gallery of Art.

➜ **Look across the street at the large red brick building.**

19 Grimké Elementary School

1925 Vermont Avenue NW

An eight-room school building (the center part of the building you see today) was first erected on this site in 1887. By 1912, it served as the business school annex to M Street High School. In 1924, it was renamed the Phelps Colored Vocational School, and in 1934, it became Grimké Elementary School. Additions were made in 1937, but the original center section is typical of the brick school buildings erected in DC in the 1880s and 1890s. The elementary school was named for Archibald H. Grimké, a lawyer, biographer, and U.S. consul to Santo Domingo. He was also the brother-in-law of Charlotte Forten Grimké and father of the Harlem Renaissance–era playwright and poet Angelina Weld Grimké.

Angelina taught English at two DC public schools, Armstrong Manual Training School and Dunbar High. Her play *Rachel* (1916) was one of the first dramas to address lynching and racial violence. Her poems appeared in anthologies and journals.

➜ **Continue north to U Street, turn right, and cross to the corner.**

19 Former site of the *Washington Eagle* Office

930 U Street

Alice Moore Dunbar-Nelson wrote poetry, fiction, and journalism and was an activist for civil rights and women's rights. She was a regular columnist for the *Washington Eagle,* the official newspaper of the Benevolent and Protective Order of Elks, from 1925 to 1930.

Dunbar-Nelson's two books are *Violets and Other Tales* (1895) and *The Goodness of St. Rocque* (1899). In addition to her journalistic work for the *Washington Eagle,* she was a regular columnist for the *Pittsburgh Courier* and coeditor of the *A.M.E. Review.* She also taught high-school English.

After her separation from her first husband, Paul Laurence Dunbar, Dunbar-Nelson remained in the area, living in Maryland and Delaware but often returning to

DC, where she was an active member of Georgia Douglas Johnson's literary salon. By the time she worked for the newspaper headquartered here, Dunbar-Nelson was married for a third and final time, to the journalist Robert J. Nelson. She always retained her eminent first husband's last name, however, as it helped her get speaking engagements and secure publication of her own work. She would split royalties from his publications with Dunbar's mother.

→ **Continue east on U Street.**

20 Former location of Murray's Palace Casino

920–922 U Street NW

This building, constructed in 1908, was home to the Murray Brothers Printing House, an African American–owned business run by the brothers Raymond, Morris, and Norman Murray, whose clients included the federal government and the *Washington Tribune*. In the 1920s, the Murray Brothers opened the upstairs as a popular dance hall, Murray Palace Casino, which could hold up to 1,800 patrons at a time.

Edward Christopher Williams published his novel *When Washington Was in Vogue* in sections in the *Messenger* (from 1925 to 1926) under the name "Letters of Davy Carr, a True Story of Colored Vanity Fair." Among other recognizable businesses active in the 1920s in the U Street neighborhood, he mentions Murray's Palace Casino in particular, as the site of a dance party.

The first African American professional librarian in the nation, Williams was principal of M Street High School before being named university librarian at

Howard. Williams is the author of three plays, all written in the 1920s: *The Exile, Sheriff's Children,* and *The Chasm.* He also wrote short stories, articles, and poems. He was an active member of a number of DC cultural societies, including the Mu-So-Lit Club, the Drama Committee of the NAACP, and the Literary Lovers. He was fluent in five languages. When he died at age fifty-eight, Williams was completing a PhD at Columbia University. *When Washington Was in Vogue* was finally published in book form in 2004. In this fast-paced and highly recommended novel set in the U Street neighborhood, not a single white person appears.

➜ **Retrace your steps west on U Street, crossing Vermont Avenue again.**

21 Garnet-Patterson Junior High School

2001 Tenth Street NW

The first school at this site was erected in 1880, when DC public schools were segregated. The current building was dedicated in 1929, combining two adjacent schools, Garnet and Patterson, and retaining both names. It honors Henry Highland Garnet, an orator and abolitionist, and James Patterson, the U.S. congressman who prepared the law establishing the Negro Public School system in DC. Notable graduates include the jazz musician Billy Taylor, DC congressional delegate Walter Fauntroy, and singers Marvin Gaye and Pearl Bailey.

Pearl Bailey was born in Virginia and spent her childhood in DC. She returned to the city in her late sixties to study theology at Georgetown University,

Prince Hall Masonic Temple

earning a bachelor's degree in 1985. She published six books about her life, education, and cooking. Bailey is best known as an actress and singer, winning Tony and Emmy awards and appearing in such films as *Carmen Jones* (1954) and *Porgy and Bess* (1959). She performed in several DC clubs during the Harlem Renaissance, including the Jungle Inn, Republic Gardens, and the Howard Theater.

22 Prince Hall Masonic Temple

1000 U Street NW

Constructed from 1922 to 1929, the Most Worshipful Prince Hall Grand Lodge was the first black Masonic order south of the Mason-Dixon Line. In addition to the lodge, the building once housed a bowling alley, ballroom, and restaurant and was an important social and cultural center during the Harlem Renaissance years and after. Prince Hall was listed on the National Register of Historic Places in 1983.

The building's architect, Albert Cassell, came from modest means but attended the architecture program at Cornell University. His studies were interrupted by service in the U.S. Army in World War I, but he completed his degree in 1919, and in 1920 he returned to the region to join the faculty of Howard University and become one of DC's first licensed African American architects. In 1922 he was named university architect and head of the Architecture Department at Howard. Over eighteen years, Cassells designed and built fourteen buildings on the Howard campus, most notably the Founders Library.

Cassell also designed buildings for the campuses of Morgan State College, Tuskegee Institute, and Virginia Union University. In DC, he designed churches, public housing complexes (including Mayfair Mansions Apartments, also listed on the National Register of Historic Places), and the Phyllis Wheatley YWCA (another NRHP building, briefly the home of Zora Neale Hurston while she was a student at Howard).

Cassell's four children also became architects. In all, the family transformed the built environment of DC, were active in civil rights, and paved the way for future generations of African American architects.

Prince Hall is also the home of the DC Branch of the NAACP. Founded in 1909, the NAACP is the oldest and largest civil rights organization in the United States, and the DC branch has always been the most active of the three hundred branches. The NAACP has led campaigns to end lynching and to integrate public schools and the military. In 1910, the NAACP inaugurated its journal, the *Crisis,* which by the 1920s became a major outlet for the creative voices of the Harlem Renaissance.

In 1920, James Weldon Johnson became the Association's first African American secretary; in this position, he significantly raised the public profile and membership of the organization. Johnson lived nearby, at 1333 R Street NW. Trained as a lawyer, he wrote novels, poems, collections of folklore, lyrics, and criticism. He edited three anthologies during his decade in DC: *The Book of American Negro Poetry* (1922) and two books of Negro spirituals (1925, 1926). He would go on to publish a memoir, two books of nonfiction, and the groundbreaking novel *The Autobiography of an Ex-Colored Man* (1912). His six books of poems include *Fifty Years and Other Poems* (1917) and *God's Trombones: Seven Negro Sermons in Verse* (1927). His song lyrics include "Lift Every Voice and Sing," sometimes referred to as the Negro National Anthem.

Johnson was later named U.S. consul to Venezuela, U.S. consul to Nicaragua, and chair of creative literature at Fisk University.

➜ **Continue east on U Street.**

23 Corner of U and Eleventh Streets

Dubbed the "Black Broadway" by singer Pearl Bailey, U Street was home to several fancy nightclubs, theaters, and restaurants that catered to the city's prosperous and proud African American middle class. Many of the buildings from the 1920s still stand. U Street had the only bank in the city that would lend to African American patrons (the Industrial Bank of Washington, still standing at 2000 Eleventh Street NW), the Hiawatha

Theater (at 2008 Eleventh Street NW, around the corner and adjoining the Industrial Bank, now razed), the first African American–owned Western Union office, Addison N. Scurlock's elite photography studio, and such clubs as the famous Bohemian Caverns (2001 Eleventh Street NW), Republic Gardens (1355 U Street NW), the Bali, the Turf Club, Club Louisiana, the Casbah, Murray's Palace Casino, the Clef Club, Phoenix Inn, and the Brass Rail.

➜ **Continue east on U Street.**

24 True Reformers Hall

1200 U Street NW

Built in 1903 as a benevolent society by the African American architect John A. Lankford, the building was purchased in 1917 by the Knights of Pythias for use as a temple. (Note the cornerstone on the Twelfth Street side.) The second-floor auditorium, seating more than two thousand people, was a popular dance hall and the site of Duke Ellington's first paid, professional gig. On the ground floor and basement levels, several African American small businesses and social clubs rented space. The basement was also used as a drill hall and armory for DC's only African American National Guard unit.

➜ **Continue east on U Street and return to the plaza where the tour began.**

25 Back at Metro Plaza

Sterling A. Brown, who would be named the first poet laureate of Washington in 1984, argued that Washington, rather than New York, was the more serious city for artists during the Harlem Renaissance. In his essay "The New Negro in Literature (1925–1955)," he wrote:

The New Negro is not to me a group of writers centered in Harlem during the second half of the twenties. Most of the writers were not Harlemites; much of the best writing was not about Harlem, which was the show-window, the cashier's till, but no more Negro American than New York is America. . . . Wa-wa trumpets, trap drums (doubling for tom-toms), and shapely dancers with bunches of bananas girdling their middles in Bamboo Inns and Jungle Cabarets nurtured tourists' delusions of "the Congo cutting through the black," . . . flattered by influential creators, critics, and publishers who had suddenly discovered the dark world at their doorstep, many Negroes helped to make a cult of Harlem. . . . [G]rafting primitivism on decadence, they typified one phase of American literary life in the twenties. . . . But several writers were uncomfortable at the racial mystique that seemed the price of the new freedom.

The heyday for this area was between the 1910s and 1940s, after which it went into a slow economic decline. The U and Fourteenth Street areas were decimated in the violent riots of 1968 following the assassination of Martin Luther King Jr. Many businesses went up in flames, and a number of old buildings had to be torn down. The neighborhood did not really begin to recover economically until the real estate boom of the 1990s. A renewed interest in historic preservation since that time has brought new investment to the area and a new interest in the Harlem Renaissance period.

Poems by Harlem Renaissance Writers

RONDEAU

Jessie Redmon Fauset

When April's here and meadows wide
Once more with spring's sweet growths are pied
    I close each book, drop each pursuit,
    And past the brook, no longer mute,
I joyous roam the countryside.

Look, here the violets shy abide
And there the mating robins hide—
    How keen my sense, how acute,
      When April's here!

And list! down where the shimmering tide
Hard by that farthest hill doth glide,
    Rise faint strains from shepherd's flute,
    Pan's pipes and Berecyntian lute.
Each sight, each sound fresh joys provide
      When April's here.

TO AMERICA

James Weldon Johnson

How would you have us, as we are?
Or sinking 'neath the load we bear?
Our eyes fixed forward on a star?
Or gazing empty at despair?

Rising or falling? Men or things?
With dragging pace or footsteps fleet?

Strong, willing sinews in your wings?
Or tightening chains about your feet?

SHADOW

Richard Bruce Nugent

Silhouette
On the face of the moon
Am I.
A dark shadow in the light.
A silhouette am I
On the face of the moon
Lacking color
Or vivid brightness
But defined all the clearer
Because
I am dark,
Black on the face of the moon.
A shadow am I
Growing in the light,
Not understood as is the day,
But more easily seen
Because
I am a shadow in the light.

Portraits

Georgia Douglas Johnson
September 10, 1880–May 14, 1966

Of all the sites associated with the Harlem Renaissance, surely one of the most significant is the home of Georgia Douglas Johnson, which still stands at 1461 S Street NW (although later owners have built a large addition at the back of the property). A gifted organizer, a generous friend, and a mentor to many, Johnson hosted her salons weekly from 1921 to approximately 1928; she continued hosting gatherings more sporadically through the Great Depression and into the early 1940s. She wrote that she named her house Half-Way House because "I'm half way between everybody and everything, and I bring them together."

Langston Hughes was a regular at these salons in the mid-1920s. In his autobiography, *The Big Sea* (1940), he wrote:

Georgia Douglas Johnson, a charming woman poet, who had two sons in college, turned her house into a salon for us on Saturday nights. . . . My two years in Washington were unhappy years, except for poetry and the friends I made through poetry. I wrote many poems. I always put them away new for several weeks in a bottom drawer. Then I would take them out and re-read them. If they seemed bad, I would throw them away. They would all seem good when I wrote them and, usually, bad when I would look at them again. So most of them were thrown away.

Georgia Douglas Johnson

Evenings consisted of discussions centered on historical and cultural topics, alternating with evenings in which writers shared and critiqued one another's work-in-progress. Johnson was an excellent leader. As Elizabeth McHenry writes in *Forgotten Readers: Recovering the Lost History of African American Literary Societies* (2002):

She took it upon herself to invite talented but undiscovered individuals she came across to participate in the Saturday Nighters' weekly meetings and did not hesitate to mention the names of those whose work she believed should receive recognition to the prominent literary figures whose influences she knew could advance their careers. . . . While the door was always open to new members, and members were welcome to bring their friends and literary colleagues to the meetings, Johnson acted decisively if she felt that a new attendee might limit the Saturday Nighters' productivity. The gentle but firm control she exerted over the group is confirmed by J. C. Byars, a Washington journalist and poet. In his 1927 anthology of Washington writers he noted that Johnson monitored those who attended her Saturday evening meetings: "If dull ones come, she weeds them out, gently, effectively. The Negro's predicament is such, Mrs. Johnson believes, that only the white people can afford to have dull leaders."

For writers, working in isolation, such community gathering sites are crucial connections. For younger writers especially, a group such as this serves as a first real audience. By taking younger writers seriously, Johnson allowed them to take themselves seriously as well. By creating this point of connection, Johnson not only helped birth the Harlem Renaissance, but she also helped to jump-start literary modernism. And this is part of her fascination, since she was not fully a modernist herself. Instead, her work serves as a bridge between older and newer writing styles and sensibilities.

In the introduction to her second book, *Bronze* (1922), she wrote this credo: "This book is the child of a bitter earth-wound. I sit on the earth and sing— sing out, and of, my sorrow. Yet, fully conscious of the potent agencies that silently work in their healing ministries, I know that God's sun shall one day shine upon a perfected and unhampered people."

Much of her work addresses love and personal relationships, and much of it is aracial. Johnson wrote in a

1941 letter to Arna Bontemps: "Whenever I can, I forget my special call to sorrow, and live as happily as I may. Perhaps that is why I seldom elect to write racially. It seems to me an art to forget those things that make the heart heavy. If one can soar, he should soar, leaving his chains behind. But, lest we forget, we must now and then come down to earth, accept the yoke and help draw the load."

Born in 1877, she married and was the mother of two sons. After her husband's death in 1925, she became the family's primary wage earner, working at a series of government jobs, including for the DC Public Schools and the U.S. Department of Labor, and selling articles to newspapers, earning enough to send both her sons to college.

She began publishing actively in 1916, prior to the start of the Harlem Renaissance period, and her first book, *The Heart of a Woman,* came out in 1918, followed by *Bronze: A Book of Verse* in 1922 and *An Autumn Love Cycle* in 1928. A final book of poems, *Share My World,* was published in 1962 near the end of her life. Her newspaper column, "Homely Philosophy," was syndicated in twenty newspapers between 1926 and 1932.

Of her third book, Alice Dunbar-Nelson wrote in her *Diary* of the daring themes: "It makes you blush at times, the baring of the inmost secrets of a soul, as it does. I wonder what Link thinks of it?" Whatever her son thought of *An Autumn Love Cycle,* its exploration of sexual love makes this book Douglas Johnson's most modernist. As Maureen Honey writes in *Aphrodite's Daughters: Three Modernist Poets of the Harlem Renaissance* (2016): "Any woman writer who highlighted erotic experience in the early twentieth century . . . took a considerable risk, but this risk was especially perilous for African Americans. Because black women were subjected to salacious stereotyping as prostitutes by the dominant culture, New Negro models of conventional femininity became firmly entrenched in black communities as a response." Perhaps Dunbar-Nelson was also shocked due to Douglas Johnson's mature age; she was forty-eight at the time of the book's release, and the love affair described in the book was the author's last major romantic attachment.

Owen Dodson wrote of her later years:

She took in anybody—old lame dogs, blind cats. . . .
Then she took in stray people—mostly artists who were out of money. People like Zora Neale Hurston who stayed there . . . or some artists who were a little bezerk. And she was capable of giving them a soothing balm. She knew how to do for people. Of course, the house was a mess! You've never been in any house like it! When you entered the hallway, you knew that you were entering another country.

Rosey E. Pool confirms that, in later years, Douglas Johnson became a hoarder. After a visit to her house in the late 1950s, she wrote: "Georgia Douglas Johnson, who now, at seventy-five, lives in Washington amidst the most chaotic amassment of usable and broken-down typewriters, television sets, radios, furniture and piles of books and papers, among which she finds any single one with unerring instinct. Her gait and talk make one think of an ancient Greek oracle."

In an undated letter to Langston Hughes (probably from 1930), Johnson wrote: "I have been fortunate in having the friendship of all of you winged artists. It has been one of my blessings. Somehow all that I have missed in the big ways of the world with its fanfare of trumpets, have more than been compensated for through the fragrant friendships I have known."

Two poems by Georgia Douglas Johnson:

THE HEART OF A WOMAN

The heart of a woman goes forth with the dawn,
As a lone bird, soft winging, so restlessly on,
Afar o'er life's turrets and vales does it roam
In the wake of those echoes the heart calls home.

The heart of a woman falls back with the night,
And enters some alien cage in its plight,
And tries to forget it has dreamed of the stars,
While it breaks, breaks, breaks on the sheltering bars.

COMMON DUST

And who shall separate the dust
What later we shall be:
Whose keen discerning eye will scan
And solve the mystery?

The high, the low, the rich, the poor,
The black, the white, the red,
And all the chromatique between,
Of whom shall it be said:

Here lies the dust of Africa;
Here are the sons of Rome;
Here lies the one unlabeled,
The world at large his home!

Can one then separate the dust?
Will mankind lie apart,
When life has settled back again
The same as from the start?

Sinclair Lewis

February 7, 1885–January 10, 1951

I don't know how you fellows feel about Prohibition, but the way it strikes me is that it's a mighty beneficial thing for the poor zob that hasn't got any will-power but for fellows like us, it's an infringement of personal liberty. —Babbitt

Sinclair Lewis, famous for novels about the small-town life in the Midwest, did his most productive writing during the period he lived in Washington, DC. He wrote his classic books *Main Street* (1920), *Babbitt* (1922), and *Arrowsmith* (1925) while living in the capital, and two of the homes he rented still stand, at 1639 Nineteenth Street NW in the Dupont Circle neighborhood and at 3028 Q Street NW in Georgetown.

The first American writer to win the Nobel Prize in Literature (1930), Lewis wrote twenty-three novels, as well as plays and short fiction. His other novels include *Elmer Gantry* (1927) and *Dodsworth* (1929), both adapted into movies, as well as *It Can't Happen Here* (1935), *Kingsblood Royal* (1947), and the posthumous *World So Wide* (1951). H. L. Mencken characterized him as a "red-haired tornado from the Minnesota wilds."

Main Street sold an estimated 2 million copies within the first few years after publication and made Lewis rich. The biographer Mark Schorer states: "It was the most sensational event in twentieth-century American publishing history. . . . The printers could not keep up with the orders, and the publishers had for a while to ration out copies to booksellers." Here is an excerpt from the penultimate chapter, set in DC:

She found employment in the Bureau of War Risk Insurance. Though the armistice with Germany was signed a

Sinclair Lewis

few weeks after her coming to Washington, the work of the bureau continued. . . . She discovered that most of the women in government bureaus lived unheathfully, dining on snatches in their crammed apartments. . . .

Washington gave her all the graciousness in which she had faith: white columns seen across leafy parks, spacious avenues, twisty alleys. Daily she passed a dark square house with a hint of magnolias and a courtyard behind it, and a tall curtained second-story window through which a woman was always peering. The woman was a mystery, romance, a story which told itself differently every day; now she was a murderess, now the neglected wife of an ambassador. . . .

As she flitted up Sixteenth Street . . . as the lamps kindled in spheres of soft fire, as the breeze flowed into the street, fresh as prairie winds and kindlier, as she glanced up the elm alley of Massachusetts Avenue, as she was rested by the integrity of the Scottish Rite Temple, she loved the city as she loved no one save Hugh. She encountered negro shanties turned into studios, with orange curtains and pots of mignonette; marble houses on New Hampshire Avenue, with butlers and limousines; and men who looked like fictional explorers and aviators. Her days were swift, and she knew that in her folly of running away she had found the courage to be wise.

She had a dispiriting first month of hunting lodgings in the crowded city. She had to roost in a hall-room in a moldy mansion conducted by an indignant decayed gentlewoman, and leave Hugh to the care of a doubtful nurse. But later she made a home. . . .

Guy Pollock wrote to a cousin, a temporary army captain. . . . The captain introduced her to the secretary of a congressman, a cynical young widow with many acquaintances in the navy. Through her Carol met commanders and majors, newspapermen, chemists and geographers and fiscal experts from the bureaus, and a teacher who was a familiar of the militant suffrage headquarters. . . . [S]he was casually adopted by this family of friendly women who, when they were not being mobbed or arrested, took dancing lessons or went picnicking up the Chesapeake Canal or talked about the politics of the American Federation of Labor.

With the congressman's secretary and the teacher Carol leased a small flat. Here she found home, her own place and her own people. . . . [C]hiefly Washington was associated with people, scores of them, sitting about the flat, talking, talking, talking, not always wisely but always excitedly. . . . She was sometimes shocked. . . . When they were most eager about soviets or canoeing, she listened, longed to have some special learning which would distinguish her, and sighed that her adventure had come so late. . . .

Most of the men who came to the flat, whether they were army officers or radicals who hated the army, had the gentleness, the acceptance of women without embarrassed banter, for which she had longed. . . . The thing she gained in Washington was not information about office-systems and labor unions but renewed courage, that amiable contempt called poise.

Jean Toomer

December 26, 1894–March 30, 1967

Jean Toomer is best known as the author of *Cane* (1923), a collection of fiction and poems set in rural Georgia and Washington, DC, widely acknowledged as one of the masterpieces of the Harlem Renaissance. He also published plays and essays. His *Collected Poems* were published posthumously in 1988.

Toomer was only twenty-eight when *Cane* was published to great critical acclaim. In an introduction to a later version of the book, Darwin T. Turner writes:

Like a nova, Toomer's literary career exploded into brilliance with *Cane,* then faded from the view of all but the few who continuously scanned the literary galaxy. Although he published a few essays, poems, and stories during more than thirty years of subsequent effort, he never again sold a book to a commercial publisher. Time, however, has restored his reputation . . . and Jean Toomer is ranked among the finest artists in the history of Afro-American literature.

Toomer was born in DC and lived in this city and New Rochelle, New York, as a child, returning to DC after his mother's death to live with his grandfather, P. B. S. Pinchback, who earlier had served as the first African American U.S. governor. He attended segregated African American public schools, Garnet Elementary and Dunbar High School. Of mixed race, Toomer later renounced racial classification, identifying only as American. He married twice, both times to white women. He studied with the spiritual leader George Ivanovich Gurdjieff in France, led Unitism communities in New York and Chicago, and later joined the Quakers.

Here are two excerpts from *Cane*.

From "Theater":

Life of nigger alleys, of pool rooms and restaurants and near-beer saloons soaks into the walls of Howard Theater and sets them throbbing jazz songs. Black-skinned, they dance and shout above the tick and trill of white-walled buildings. At night, they open doors to people who come in to stamp their feet and shout. At night, road-shows volley songs into the mass-heart of black people. Songs soak the walls and seep out to the nigger life of alleys and near-beer saloons, of the Poodle Dog and Black Bear cabarets. Afternoons, the house is dark, and the walls are sleeping singers until rehearsal begins. . . . A pianist slips into the pit and improvises jazz. The walls awake. Arms of the girls, and their limbs, which . . . jazz, jazz . . . by lifting up their tight street skirts they set free, jab the air and clog the floor in rhythm to the music. (Lift your skirts, Baby, and talk to papa!)

From "Avey":

I have a spot in Soldier's Home to which I always go when I want the simple beauty of another's soul. Robins spring about the lawn all day. They leave their footprints in the grass. I imagine that the grass at night smells sweet and fresh because of them. The ground is high. Washington lies below. Its light spreads like a blush against the darkened sky. Against the soft dusk sky of Washington. And when the wind is from the South, soil of my homeland falls like a fertile shower upon the lean streets of the city. Upon my hill in Soldier's Home. I know the policeman who watches the place of nights. When I go there alone, I talk to him. I tell him I come to there to find the truth that people bury in their hearts. I tell him that I do not come there with a girl to do the thing he's paid to watch out for. I look deep into his eyes when I say these things, and he believes me. He comes over to see who it is on the grass. I say hello to him. He greets me in the same way and goes off searching for other black splotches on the lawn. Avey and I went there. . . . I described her my own nature and temperament. Told how they needed a larger life for their expression. How incapable Washington was of understanding that need. How it could not meet it. . . . I talked, beautifully I thought, about an art that would be born, an art that would open the way for women the likes of her.

Zora Neale Hurston

January 7, 1891–January 28, 1960

Like Langston Hughes, Duke Ellington, and so many other artists of the Harlem Renaissance period, Hurston began her career in DC. May Miller (the daughter of Dean Kelly Miller) would become a famous playwright and, in her later years, a poet. Miller met Hurston in Baltimore in 1918 and convinced her to apply to Howard University, which Hurston called "the capstone of Negro education in the world." Miller told Hurston she was "Howard material." Hurston attended

Zora Neale Hurston beating the hountar, or mama drum

Howard from 1919 through 1924. She earned an associate's degree and was active in campus life. She joined a sorority, was a member of the campus theater group, and wrote for the campus literary journal, the *Stylus,* where her first short story was published. In 1943, the college gave her a Distinguished Alumni Award.

Hurston was born in 1891, but she regularly gave her age as at least ten years younger. It appears she started the practice while living in Baltimore, in order to be eligible for free public schooling, open to students aged six to twenty. In 1917, when she first enrolled in high school, she was twenty-six years old. But as Phoeby says of Janie, the main character in *Their Eyes Were Watching God,* "The worst thing Ah ever knowed her to do was taking a few years offa her age and dat ain't never harmed nobody."

Hurston, who owned only one dress when she first arrived in DC, appreciated the opportunity for an entrée into the city's elite, middle-class life. She enjoyed shopping on U Street, and her job as a manicurist soon allowed her to afford it. She wrote to Langston Hughes in 1931: "What do you think I was doing in Washington all that time if not getting cultured. I got my foot in society just as well as the rest."

At first, Hurston worked as a manicurist in George Robinson's Barbershop, an African American-owned business that catered to an all-white clientele. Hurston took classes in the mornings, then worked from 3:30 to 8:30 p.m. She later took a better-paying job as a waitress for the Cosmos Club, a private, white men's club then located in the historic Dolley Madison House on Lafayette Square.

While in DC, Hurston met Langston Hughes, and in the second half of the 1920s, this friendship was one of the most important in Hurston's life. Hurston and Hughes collaborated on a New York literary journal called *Fire!!* (along with Wallace Thurman, Aaron Douglas, Richard Bruce Nugent, Gwendolyn Bennett, and John P. Davis) in 1926. They traveled through the South together in 1927, making stops in Georgia and Alabama, including trips to Jean Toomer's ancestral home, to hear a Bessie Smith concert, and to give guest lectures to students at Tuskegee Institute. In 1928, although strapped for cash herself, Hurston lent Hughes money and gave readings of his poetry to help him sell books. But this fruitful and intense friendship was changed forever over a play, *Mule Bone,* which Hurston and Hughes wrote together in 1930. Hurston later disputed Hughes's rights to coauthorship, even consulting a lawyer. Hurston's biographer, Robert Hemenway, calls this "the most notorious literary quarrel in African-American cultural history." Although they continued to correspond after this falling-out, their friendship would never be the same.

Hurston also developed an important friendship with Georgia Douglas Johnson and was a regular in the Saturday Nighters Club. This friendship would last the rest of her life. In 1950, Hurston returned to Johnson's home for a month-long visit.

Hurston moved to New York City, earning a degree in anthropology from Barnard College (where she was the only African American student) in 1927. Hurston specialized in southern African American folk culture, a field that had, up to that point, been little studied. A timely grant in 1927 from the Association for the Study of Negro Life and History, based in Washington, allowed Hurston to continue her anthropological research into African American folk stories, music, and religious rituals in Florida, which led to the publication of her second book, *Mules and Men* (1935). She wrote to Carl Sandburg: "I am an anthropologist and it is my job to see and to find and to present to the world my findings. I have seen extracts from *Mules and Men* printed in many languages, proving that I did a fairly good job. I have never expected to get rich, and if I have served this nation and the world by digging out a few of its hidden treasures and thus enriched our culture, I have gained a great deal. I have had some influence on my time."

She is the author of four novels, most notably *Their Eyes Were Watching God* (1937), as well as two books of folklore and an autobiography, *Dust Tracks on a Road*

(1942). But by the end of the 1940s, Hurston was broke and nearly forgotten, living in Florida. When she died at age sixty-nine in 1960, her neighbors took up a collection to pay for her funeral. There was not enough money left over for a headstone, so her grave remained unmarked until 1973, when the writer Alice Walker paid for a grave marker.

In a letter to Annie Nathan Meyer dated January 1926, Hurston wrote:

Oh, if you knew my dreams! my vaulting ambition! How I constantly live in fancy in seven league boots, taking mighty strides across the world, but conscious all the time of being a mouse on a treadmill. . . . The eagerness, the burning within, I wonder sparks do not fly so that they be seen by all men. Prometheus on his rock with his liver being continually consumed as fast as he grows another, is nothing to my dreams. I dream such wonderfully complete ones, so radiant in astral beauty. I have not the power yet to make them come true. They always die. But even as they fade, I have others.

Hurston married twice, but both unions were short-lived. She wrote her first ex-husband (by then a friend and a successful physician living in Los Angeles) in 1953, toward the end of her life: "It is interesting to see how far we both have come since we did our dreaming together in Washington, D.C. We struggled so hard to make our big dreams come true, didn't we? The world has gotten some benefits from us, though we had a swell time too. We lived!"

Here is an excerpt from Hurston's essay, "How It Feels to Be Colored Me," published in 1928:

I am not tragically colored. There is no great sorrow dammed up in my soul, nor lurking behind my eyes. I do not mind at all. I do not belong to the sobbing school of Negrohood who hold that nature somehow has given them a lowdown dirty deal and whose feelings are all hurt about it. Even in the helter-skelter skirmish that is my life, I have seen that the world is to the strong regardless of a little pigmentation more or less. No, I do not weep at the world—I am too busy sharpening my oyster knife.

Someone is always at my elbow reminding me that I am the granddaughter of slaves. It fails to register depression with me. Slavery is sixty years in the past. The operation was successful and the patient is doing well, thank you. The terrible struggle that made me an American out of a potential slave said "On the line!" The Reconstruction said "Get set!" and the generation before said "Go!" I am off to a flying start and I must not halt in the stretch to look behind and weep. Slavery is the price I paid for civilization, and the choice was not with me. It is a bully adventure and worth all that I have paid through my ancestors for it. No one on earth ever had a greater chance for glory. The world to be won and nothing to be lost. It is thrilling to think—to know that for any act of mine, I shall get twice as much praise or twice as much blame. It is quite exciting to hold the center of the national stage, with the spectators not knowing whether to laugh or to weep. . . .

I have no separate feeling about being an American citizen and colored. I am merely a fragment of the Great Soul that surges within the boundaries. My country, right or wrong.

Sometimes, I feel discriminated against, but it does not make me angry. It merely astonishes me. How can any deny themselves the pleasure of my company? It's beyond me.

Selected Bibliography

Adams, Henry. *Democracy*. New York: Henry Holt, 1880.

———. *The Education of Henry Adams*. Boston: Houghton Mifflin, 1918.

———. *Esther*. New York: Henry Holt, 1884.

———. *Mont-Saint-Michel and Chartres*. Boston: Houghton Mifflin, 1904.

Alcott, Louisa May. *Hospital Sketches*. Edited by Bessie Z. Jones. Cambridge: Belknap Press of Harvard University Press, 1960.

Alexander, Eleanor. *Lyrics of Sunshine and Shadow: The Tragic Courtship and Marriage of Paul Laurence Dunbar and Alice Ruth Moore*. New York: New York University Press, 2001.

Allen, Gay Wilson. *The Solitary Singer: A Critical Biography of Walt Whitman*. New York: Macmillan, 1955.

Aloi, Daniel. "Building on Opportunity: The Cassell Family of Architects." *Ezra: Cornell's Quarterly Magazine* 7, no. 1 (Fall 2014): 24–25.

Apelbaum, Laura Cohen, and Claire Uziel. *Jewish Life in Mr. Lincoln's City*. Washington, DC: Jewish Historical Society of Greater Washington, 2009.

Beauchamp, Tanya Edwards, and Kimberly Prothro Williams. *The Anacostia Historic District*. Rev. ed. Washington, DC: Historical Society of Washington, DC, 2006.

Belasco Theater Scrapbook. Gelman Library, George Washington University Libraries.

Bernard, Emily, ed. *Remember Me to Harlem: The Letters of Langston Hughes and Carl Van Vechten*. New York: Vintage, 2001.

Bethel Literary and Historical Society Papers. Moorland-Spingarn Collection, Howard University Libraries, Washington, DC.

Bierce, Ambrose. *The Collected Writings of Ambrose Bierce*. Edited by Clifton Fadiman. New York: Citadel, 1946.

———. *The Letters of Ambrose Bierce*. Edited by Bertha Clark Pope. San Francisco: Book Club of California, 1922.

Boyd, Valerie. *Wrapped in Rainbows: A Biography of Zora Neale Hurston.* London: Virago, 2003.

Brawley, Benjamin. *Paul Laurence Dunbar: Poet of His People.* Chapel Hill: University of North Carolina Press, 1936.

Brooks, Noah. *Washington, D.C. in Lincoln's Time.* Chicago: Quadrangle, 1971.

Brown, Solomon G. *Kind Regards of Solomon G. Brown.* Washington, DC: Smithsonian Institution Press, 1983.

Brownstein, Elizabeth Smith. *Lincoln's Other White House: The Untold Story of the Man and His Presidency.* Hoboken, NJ: Wiley, 2005.

Burnett, Frances Hodgson. *Through One Administration.* Ridgewood, NJ: Gregg, 1886.

Burroughs, John. *Wake-Robin.* New York: Hurd and Houghton, 1871.

Cader, Harold Dean, ed. *Henry Adams and His Friends: A Collection of His Unpublished Letters.* Boston: Houghton Mifflin, 1947.

Callow, Philip. *From Noon to Starry Night: A Life of Walt Whitman.* Chicago: Dee, 1992.

Cary, Francine Curro, ed. *Washington Odyssey: A Multicultural History of the Nation's Capital.* Washington, DC: Smithsonian Books, 1996.

Clark-Lewis, Elizabeth, ed. *First Freed: Washington, D.C., in the Emancipation Era.* Washington, DC: Howard University Press, 2002.

Cooper, Anna Julia, ed. *The Life and Writings of the Grimké Family.* Privately printed, 1951.

———. *A Voice from the South,* 1892.

Cullen, Countee, ed. *Caroling Dusk: An Anthology of Verse by Negro Poets,* New York: Harper and Row, 1955.

Douglass, Frederick. *A Lecture on Our National Capital.* Exhibition catalogue. Anacostia Neighborhood Museum. Washington, DC: Smithsonian Institution Press, 1978.

———. *Narrative of the Life of Frederick Douglass, an American Slave: Written by Himself.* Boston: Anti-Slavery Office, 1845.

Paul Laurence Dunbar Collection. Dayton Metro Library, Dayton, OH.

Dunbar, Paul Laurence. *The Collected Poetry of Paul Laurence Dunbar.* Edited by Joanne M. Braxton. Charlottesville: University of Virginia Press, 1993.

Alice Dunbar-Nelson Papers, 1895–1942. University of Delaware Library, Newark.

Dunbar-Nelson, Alice. *Give Us Each Day: The Diary of Alice Dunbar-Nelson.* Edited by Gloria T. Hull. New York: Norton, 1984.

———. *The Goodness of St. Rocque and Other Stories.* New York: Dodd, Mead, 1899.

———. *Violets and Other Tales.* Boston: Monthly Review, 1895.

Dykstra, Natalie. *Clover Adams: A Gilded and Heartbreaking Life.* Boston: Houghton Mifflin Harcourt, 2012.

Epstein, Daniel Mark. *Lincoln and Whitman: Parallel Lives in Civil War Washington.* New York: Ballantine, 2004.

Erkkila, Betsy. *Whitman: The Political Poet.* New York: Oxford University Press, 1989.

Fauset, Jessie Redmon. *Plum Bun: A Novel without a Moral.* New York: Frederick A. Stokes 1928.

———. *There Is Confusion.* Boston: Northeastern University Press, 1924.

The Charles E. Feinberg Collection of the Papers of Walt Whitman. Library of Congress, Washington, DC.

Fitzpatrick, Sandra, and Maria R. Goodwin. *The Guide to Black Washington.* Rev. ed. New York: Hippocrene, 1999.

Fogle, Jeanne. *Proximity to Power: Neighbors to the Presidents near Lafayette Square.* Washington, DC: Tour de Force, 1999.

Folsom, Ed, ed. *Walt Whitman: The Centennial Essays.* Iowa City: University of Iowa Press, 1994.

Friedrich, Otto. *Clover.* New York: Simon and Schuster, 1979.

Furgurson, Ernest B. *Freedom Rising: Washington in the Civil War.* New York: Knopf, 2004.

Gardner, Alexander. *Gardner's Photographic Sketch Book of the War.* Vols. 1 and 2. Washington, DC: Philp and Solomons, 1865, 1866.

Gatewood, Willard B. *Aristocrats of Color: The Black Elite, 1880–1920.* Fayetteville: University of Arkansas Press, 2000.

Gelderman, Carol. *A Free Man of Color and His Hotel: Race, Reconstruction, and the Role of the Federal Government.* Washington, DC: Potomac Books, 2012.

Gelman Library Special Collections Department, George Washington University. *Washington, D.C. Fiction: A Bibliography of the Holdings of Special Collections in the Gelman Library,* 2007.

Genoways, Ted. *Walt Whitman and the Civil War: America's Poet during the Lost Years of 1860–1862.* Berkeley: University of California Press, 2009.

Green, Constance McLaughlin. *The Secret City: A History of Race Relations in the Nation's Capital.* Princeton, NJ: Princeton University Press, 1967.

Greenspan, Ezra, ed. *The Cambridge Companion to Walt Whitman,* Cambridge: University of Cambridge Press, 1995.

Harris, Leonard, and Charles Molesworth. *Alain L. Locke: The Biography of a Philosopher.* Chicago: University of Chicago Press, 2008.

Hemenway, Robert E. *Zora Neale Hurston: A Literary Biography.* Urbana: University of Illinois Press, 1977.

Honey, Maureen. *Aphrodite's Daughters: Three Modernist Poets of the Harlem Renaissance.* New Brunswick, NJ: Rutgers University Press, 2016.

Hughes, Langston. *The Big Sea: An Autobiography.* New York: Knopf, 1940.

———. *The Collected Poems of Langston Hughes.* Edited by Arnold Rampersad. New York: Vintage, 1995.

———. *Fine Clothes to the Jew.* New York: Knopf, 1927.

———. *Weary Blues.* New York: Knopf, 1926.

Hull, Gloria T. *Color, Sex and Poetry: Three Women Writers of the Harlem Renaissance.* Bloomington: Indiana University Press, 1987.

Hunter, Alfred. *The Washington and Georgetown Directory.* Kirkwood & McGill, various years.

Hurston, Lucy Anne, and the Estate of Zora Neale Hurston. *Speak, So You Can Speak Again: The Life of Zora Neale Hurston.* New York: Doubleday, 2004.

Hurston, Zora Neale. *Dust Tracks on a Road: An Autobiography.* New York: Lippincott, 1942.

———. "How It Feels to Be Colored Me." *World Tomorrow* 11 (May 1928): 215–16.

———. *Mules and Men.* New York: Lippincott, 1935.

———. *Their Eyes Were Watching God.* New York: Lippincott, 1937.

Johnson, Georgia Douglas. *An Autumn Love Cycle.* New York: Vinal, 1928.

———. *Bronze: A Book of Verse.* Boston: Brimmer, 1922.

———. *The Heart of a Woman and Other Poems.* Boston: Cornhill 1918.

Jones, Sharon L. *Rereading the Harlem Renaissance: Race, Class, and Gender in the Fiction of Jessie Fauset, Zora Neale Hurston, and Dorothy West.* Westport, CT: Greenwood, 2002.

Kaplan, Carla, ed. *Zora Neale Hurston: A Life in Letters.* New York: Anchor, 2003.

Kaplan, Justin. *Walt Whitman: A Life.* New York: Perennial, 2003.

Katz, D. Mark. *Witness to an Era: The Life and Photographs of Alexander Gardner.* New York: Viking, 1991.

Kreig, Joann P. *A Whitman Chronology.* Iowa City: University of Iowa Press, 1998.

Leech, Margaret. *Reveille in Washington, 1860–1865.* New York: Harper and Brothers, 1941.

LeMaster, J. R., and Donald D. Cummings, eds, *Walt Whitman: An Encyclopedia,* New York: Garland, 1998.

Lewis, Sinclair. *Babbitt.* New York: Harcourt, Brace, 1922.

———. *Main Street.* New York: Harcourt, Brace, 1920.

Lewis, Tom. *Washington: A History of Our National City.* New York: Basic, 2015.

Loving, Jerome. *Walt Whitman: The Song of Himself.* Berkeley: University of California Press, 1999.

Lowenfels, Walter, ed. *Walt Whitman's Civil War.* New York: Da Capo, 1960.

Luria, Sarah. *Capital Speculations: Writing and Building Washington, D.C.* Hanover, NH: University Press of New England, 2006.

McHenry, Elizabeth. *Forgotten Readers: Recovering the Lost History of African American Literary Societies.* Durham, NC: Duke University Press, 2002.

McQuirter, Marya Annette. *African American Heritage Trail, Washington, DC*. Washington, DC: Cultural Tourism DC, 2003.

Miller, Matt. *Collage of Myself: Walt Whitman and the Making of Leaves of Grass*. Lincoln: University of Nebraska Press, 2010.

Mills, Cynthia. *Beyond Grief: Sculpture and Wonder in the Gilded Age Cemetery*. Washington, DC: Smithsonian Institution Scholarly Press, 2014.

Moore, Jacqueline M. *Leading the Race: The Transformation of the Black Elite in the Nation's Capital, 1880–1920*. Charlottesville: University Press of Virginia, 1999.

Morely, Jefferson. *Snow-Storm in August: Washington City, Francis Scott Key, and the Forgotten Race Riot of 1835*. New York: Nan A. Talese/Doubleday, 2012.

Morris, Roy, Jr. *The Better Angel: Walt Whitman in the Civil War*. New York: Oxford University Press, 2001.

Muller, John H. *Mark Twain in Washington: The Adventures of a Capital Correspondent*. Charleston, SC: History Press, 2013.

Murray, Martin G. "'Pete the Great': A Biography of Peter Doyle." *Walt Whitman Quarterly Review* 12 (Summer 1994): 1–51.

———. "Traveling with the Wounded: Walt Whitman and Washington's Civil War Hospitals." *Washington History* 8 (Fall/Winter 1996–97): 58–73.

Myerson, Joel, ed. *Whitman in His Own Time*. Iowa City: University of Iowa Press, 1991.

O'Connor, William Douglas. *The Good Gray Poet: A Vindication*. New York: Bunce & Huntington, 1866.

O'Toole, Patricia. *The Five of Hearts: An Intimate Portrait of Henry Adams and His Friends 1880–1918*. New York: Ballantine, 1990.

Peabody, Richard, ed. *D.C. Magazines: A Literary Retrospective*. Washington, DC: Paycock, 1981.

Perry, Mark, *Lift up Thy Voice: The Grimké Family's Journey from Slaveholders to Civil Rights Leaders*. New York: Penguin, 2001.

Pollak, Vivian R. *The Erotic Whitman*. Berkeley: University of California Press, 2000.

Pool, Rosey E. *Beyond the Blues.* London: Hand and Flower, 1962.

Price, Kenneth M. *To Walt Whitman, America.* Chapel Hill: University of North Carolina Press, 2004.

———, ed. *Walt Whitman: The Contemporary Reviews.* Cambridge: Cambridge University Press, 1996.

———. *Whitman and Tradition: The Poet in His Century.* New Haven, CT: Yale University Press, 1990.

Renehan, Edward J., Jr. "Burroughs and Whitman: Comrades in Letters and Life." Vassar College Libraries, Archives and Special Collections. Web exhibit, *Walt Whitman & John Burroughs: Literary Comrades,* 2008. https://specialcollections.vassar.edu/exhibit-highlights/2006-2010/burroughs_whitman/edward_renehan.html.

Reynolds, David S., ed. *A Historical Guide to Walt Whitman,* New York: Oxford University Press, 2000.

———. *Walt Whitman: Lives and Legacies.* New York: Oxford University Press, 2005.

Roberts, Kim, "The Bethel Literary and Historical Society." *Beltway Poetry Quarterly* 11 (Spring 2010): http://washingtonart.com/beltway/bethel.html.

———. "D.C.'s Big Read: Zora Neale Hurston's Washington." Humanities Council of Washington, DC, 2007.

———. "Georgia Douglas Johnson." *Beltway Poetry Quarterly* 13 (Fall 2012): www.beltwaypoetry.com/georgia-douglas-johnson/.

———. "Langston Hughes in Washington, DC: Conflict and Class." *Beltway Poetry Quarterly* 12 (Winter 2011): http://washingtonart.com/beltway/hughes2.html.

———. "Walt Whitman, Civil War Nurse." *American Journal of Medicine* 118 (July 2005): 787.

———. "Whitman in Washington (1863–1873)." *Beltway Poetry Quarterly* 4 (Fall 2003): http://washingtonart.com/beltway/whitman.html.

Roberts, Kim, and Martin G. Murray. "Whitman in DC: Gay DC Walking Tours." Rainbow History Project, 2005.

Roberts, Kim, and Dan Vera. *DC Writers' Homes.* Web exhibit, 2011, with regular updates. www.dcwriters.org.

Robertson, Michael, *Worshipping Walt: The Whitman Disciples,* Princeton, NJ: Princeton University Press, 2008.

Roper, Robert. *Now the Drum of War: Walt Whitman and His Brothers in the Civil War.* New York: Walker, 2008.

Roses, Lorraine Elena, and Ruth Elizabeth Randolph. *Harlem Renaissance and Beyond: Literary Biographies of 100 Black Women Writers, 1900–1945.* Cambridge: Harvard University Press, 1990.

———, eds. *Harlem's Glory: Black Women Writing, 1900–1950.* Cambridge: Harvard University Press, 1996.

Samuels, Ernest. *Henry Adams.* 1964. Cambridge: Harvard University Press, 1989.

Sandweiss, Martha A. *Passing Strange: A Gilded Tale of Love and Deception across the Color Line.* New York: Penguin, 2009.

Schaffner, M. A. "A Good Opinion of Bierce." *Beltway Poetry Quarterly* 9 (Summer 2008): http://washingtonart.com/ beltway/bierce.html.

Scheyer, Ernst. *The Circle of Henry Adams: Art & Artist.* Detroit: Wayne State University Press, 1970.

Schmidgall, Gary, ed. *Intimate with Walt: Selections from Whitman's Conversations with Horace Traubel, 1888–1892.* Iowa City: University of Iowa Press, 2001.

———. *Walt Whitman: A Gay Life.* New York: Dutton, 1997.

Schorer, Mark. *Sinclair Lewis: An American Life.* New York: McGraw-Hill, 1961.

Shively, Charley, ed. *Drum Beats: Walt Whitman's Civil War Boy Lovers.* San Francisco: Gay Sunshine, 1989.

Simmons, William J. *Men of Mark: Eminent, Progressive and Rising,* Cleveland: Rewell, 1887.

Stearns, Amanda Akin. *The Lady Nurse of Ward E.* New York: Baker and Taylor, 1909.

Taylor, Benjamin Ogle, *Our Neighbors on La Fayette Square.* Washington, DC: Privately printed, 1872.

Taylor, Elizabeth Dowling. *The Original Black Elite: Daniel Murray and the Story of a Forgotten Era.* New York: HarperCollins, 2017.

———. *A Slave in the White House: Paul Jennings and the Madisons,* New York: Palgrave Macmillan, 2012.

Terrell, Mary Church. *A Colored Woman in a White World.* Washington, DC: Ransdell, 1940.

Toomer, Jean. *Cane.* New York: Liveright, 1923.

Tracy, Steven C. *A Historical Guide to Langston Hughes.* New York: Oxford University Press, 2004.

Twain, Mark, and Charles Dudley Warner. *The Gilded Age.* Hartford City, IN: American Publishing, 1874.

Voss, Frederick S. *Majestic in His Wrath: A Pictorial Life of Frederick Douglass.* Washington, DC: Smithsonian Institution Press, 1995.

Walker, Cheryl, ed. *American Women Poets of the Nineteenth Century: An Anthology.* New Brunswick, NJ: Rutgers University Press, 1992

Watson, Steven. *The Harlem Renaissance: Hub of African-American Culture, 1920–1930.* New York: Pantheon, 1995.

West, Aberjhani, and Sandra L. West. *Encyclopedia of the Harlem Renaissance.* New York: Checkmark, 2003.

Whitman, Walt. *The Correspondence of Walt Whitman.* Edited by Edwin Haviland Miller. 5 vols. New York: New York University Press, 1961.

———. *Memoranda during the War.* Edited by Peter Coviello. Oxford: Oxford University Press, 2004.

———. *Walt Whitman: Complete Poetry and Collected Prose.* New York: Library of America, 1982.

Williams, Edward Christopher. *When Washington Was in Vogue: A Lost Novel of the Harlem Renaissance.* Edited by Adam McKible. New York: Harper Perennial, 2005.

Williams, Lida Keck. *The Life and Works of Paul Laurence Dunbar.* Washington, DC: Austin Jenkins, 1907.

Willis, Garry. *Henry Adams and the Making of America.* Boston: Houghton Mifflin, 2005.

Woodress, James. *A Yankee's Odyssey: The Life of Joel Barlow.* Philadelphia: Lippincott, 1958.

Wright, Richard R. *Centennial Encyclopaedia of the African Methodist Episcopal Church.* Philadelphia: Book Concern of the A.M.E. Church, 1916.

Wylie, Elinor. *Collected Poems of Elinor Wylie.* New York: Knopf, 1932.

Yale Collection of American Literature. Beinecke Rare Book and Manuscript Library, Yale University, New Haven, CT.

Illustration Credits

Index

Italicized page numbers refer to illustrations.

Adams, Charles Francis, 119, 142
Adams, Henry *118*, 119–45; correspondence, 122, 127, 128, 131, 136, 139, 143, 144; *Democracy*, *123*; *The Education of Henry Adams*, 119, 122, 125–26, 132–33, 139, 142–43; *Esther*, 125, 128; Five of Hearts, 123, 126; "The Great Secession Winter," 142–43; *Mont-Saint-Michel and Chartres*, 127, 132
Adams, John Quincy, 138
Adams, Louisa, 119
Adams, Marion "Clover" Hooper, 122–23, 128–29, 132, 136, 143–45; correspondence, 122
Alcott, Louisa May, 4
Aldrich, Thomas Bailey, 4, 42
Alexander, Eleanor, 88; *Lyrics of Sunshine and Shadow*, 88–89
American Negro Academy, 5, 70
American Orchestra Club, 93
Andrew Jackson Sculpture, Lafayette Park (Clark Mills), *33*, 33–35, 133–34
architects and developers: Amzi L. Barber, 82; Albert Cassell, 186; Isaiah T. Hatton, 80, 176; John Lankford, 188; Benjamin Henry Latrobe, 126; John Whitelaw Lewis, 176; Mihran Mesrobian, 133; James H. McGill, 82, 95; Uriah H. Painter, 136; W. Sidney Pittman, 178; H. H. Richardson, 130–31; William Thornton, 20; Henry Wardman, 133; Sanford White, 145
Arena Stage, 169
Arlington National Cemetery, 84
Armory Square Hospital, 46–47
Armstrong, Louis, 169, 177

Armstrong Technical High School/Armstrong Manual Training School, 83, 165, 182
Art Club, 69
Arts Club of Washington, 142–43
Association for the Study of Negro Life and History, 5, 159, 164–65, 206
Atzerodt, George, 35
Aulic, John H., 19

Bachelor-Benedict Club, 90
Bailey, Pearl, 80, 184–85, 187
Baird, Spenser Fullerton, 62–63, 134
Bancroft, George, 129
banks: Capital Savings Bank, 84; Freedman's Savings Bank/Freedman's Savings and Trust Company, *36*, 36–37, 93; Industrial Bank, 64, 187–88
Barber, Amzi L., 82; LeDroit Park neighborhood, *76–77*, 82–83, 85, *87*, 96, 99, 102, 162, 178
Barlow, Joel, 4, 11–13, *12*; *The Columbiad*, 12–13
Barrymore, Ethel, 138
bars and nightclubs: Bohemian Caverns, 188; Brass Rail, 188; Casbah, 188; Clef Club, 188; Club Bali, 169, 188; Club Louisiana, 188; Lincoln Colonnade, 162; Murray's Palace Casino, 183–84, 188; Music Box/Jungle Inn, 164, 185; Phoenix Inn, 188; Republic Gardens, 185, 188; Stage Door Canteen/Lafayette Square Club, 138; Turf Club, 188
Barton, Clara, 4, 45
Becketts Cemetery, 22

Belasco, David, 138
Benét, William Rose, 152
Bennett, Gwendolyn, 205
Bernhardt, Sarah, 138
Berry, Levy Wood, 21
Bierce, Ambrose, 149–52, *150*;
    correspondence, 151; *The Devil's*
    Dictionary, 149, 151; "A Year's
    Casualties," 151–52
Birney, William, 95
Blaine, James G., 123
Blair, Montgomery, 141
Bohemian Caverns, 188
Bonaparte, Napoléon, 4, 11
Bonner, Marita, 170
Bontemps, Arna, 174, 195
Booklovers, 70
Booth, John Wilkes, 35
Botta, Anne Lynch, *23*, 23–26; "To
    an Astronomer," 24; "Webster,"
    24–26
Bowen, Arthur, 20–22
Bradley, William A., 21
Brass Rail, 188
Brawley, Benjamin, 90; *Paul Lau-*
    rence Dunbar, 90–91, 99–100
Brown, Solomon G., 5, 59–67, *60;*
    "Dear Friends, What's Aroused
    You?," 65–67; "He Is a Negro
    Still," 59; "Fifty Years Today," 63;
    Kind Regards of S. G. Brown, 61;
    "Time Dealing with Man," 67
Brown, Sterling A., 189; "The New
    Negro in Literature (1925–
    1955)," 189
Brownstein, Elizabeth Smith, 67;
    Lincoln's Other White House, 67
Bryant, William Cullen, 24
Bureau of Indian Affairs, 49–50
Burnett, Frances Hodgson, 111–
    15, *112; Through One Adminis-*
    tration, 113–15
Burrill, Mary P., 95
Burroughs Elementary School, 56
Burroughs, John, 4, 54–59, *55;*
    correspondence, 54; "Spring at
    the Capital with an Eye to the
    Birds," 56–59

Callow, Philip, 40; *From Noon to*
    Starry Night, 40
Capital Savings Bank, 84
Caldwell, Bennie, 169
Calloway, Cab, 176–77
Cameron, Elizabeth, 135–36, *137*
Cameron, J. Donald, 135–36, *137*
Caruso, Enrico, 138
Carver, George Washington, 176
Cary, Mary Ann Shadd, 5
Casbah, 188
Cassell, Albert, 186
Cater, Harold Dean, 130–31
Cedar Hill (Frederick Douglass
    National Historic Site), 105–6
cemeteries: Arlington National
    Cemetery, 84; Becketts Cem-
    etery, 22; Congressional Cem-
    etery, 22; Oak Hill Cemetery,
    95; Mt. Olivet Cemetery, 15;
    Rock Creek Church Cemetery,
    143–45, *144*
churches: Fifteenth Street Pres-
    byterian Church, 63, 68; Israel
    Bethel Colored Methodist
    Episcopal Church, 17–18, 65;
    Metropolitan African Meth-
    odist Episcopal Church, 18;
    New York Avenue Presbyterian
    Church, 34; St. John's Episco-
    pal Church, 34, 126–27, *127*
Civil War hospitals: Armory
    Square Hospital, 46–47; Patent
    Office Hospital, 45–46, *46*
Clay, Henry, 23, 134
Clef Club, 188
Cleveland, Grover, 139
clubs and associations: American
    Negro Academy, 5, 70; Amer-
    ican Orchestra Club, 93; Art
    Club, 69; Arts Club of Wash-
    ington, 142–43; Bachelor-Ben-
    edict Club, 90; Booklovers, 70;
    Colored Women's League, 69;
    Cosmos Club, 134–35, *135, 137,*
    138, 205; Evenings at Home,
    93; Hillsdale Pioneer Associa-
    tion, 64; Literary Lovers, 184;

Metropolitan Club, 141; Monday Night Literary Society, 90; Mu-So-Lit Club, 184; National Association of College Women, 98; National Association of Colored Women, 69; National Association of Colored Women's Clubs, 98; National Geographic Society, 135, 137; Pen and Pencil Club, 90; Prince Hall Masonic Temple, 185, 185–86

Club Bali, 169, 188

Club Louisiana, 188

Colored Women's League, 69, 97

Congressional Cemetery, 22

Cooper, Anna Julia, 5, 95, 96, 96–97

Corcoran Gallery of Art, 140, 181

Corcoran Office Building, 38–39

Corcoran, William, 124, 128, 140, 141

Cosmos Club, 134–35, 135, 137, 138, 205

Crisis, 174, 187

Crummell, Alexander, 5; American Negro Academy, 5

Cullen, Countee, 174

Cuney, William Waring, 170

Davis, John P., 205

DC Board of Education, 98

DC Historic Preservation Office, 64; *Anacostia Historic District*, 64–65

Decatur House, 34

Decatur, Stephen, 134

Dodson, Owen, 196

Dolley Madison House, 34, 134, 135, 205

Douglas, Aaron, 205

Douglass, Anna Murray, 107

Douglass, Frederick, 5, 37, 105–11, *106*; "A Lecture on Our National Capitol," 107–11; "The Meaning of July Fourth for the Negro," 105; *A Narrative of the Life of Frederick Douglass, An American Slave*, 105

Douglass, Helen Pitts, 107

Douglass Bridge, 107

Doyle, Peter, 39, 44

Drew, Charles, 178

Drinkard, William, 39

Du Bois, W. E. B., 165

Dunbar, Paul Laurence, 5, 74, 75–104, 182; correspondence, 88, 90; "Lover's Lane," 102–4; "Negro Society in Washington," 83, 91–92

Dunbar Hotel, 79

Dunbar-Nelson, Alice Moore, 5, 74, 75–104, 170, 182–83, 195; diary, 78, 195; "Sonnet," 104

Dunbar Theater, 78–80, *79*

Eastern Market, 17

Eaton, David, 19

Eldridge, Charles, 39

Ellington, Duke, 80, 94, 172–73, 188, 203

Emerson, Ralph Waldo, 24, 54

Etheridge, John, 19

Evanti, Madame Lillian (Lillian Evans Tibbs), 180–81

Evarts, William, 123

Evenings at Home, 93

Fauntroy, Walter, 184

Fauset, Jessie Redmon, 170, 171, 173–74, 180, 190; "Rondeau," 190

Fifteenth Street Presbyterian Church, 63, 68

Fillmore, Millard, 34

Fire!!, 205

Fitzgerald, Ella, 80

Fitzpatrick, Sandra, and Maria R. Goodwin, 167; *The Guide to Black Washington*, 167, 180

Fleetwood, Christian A., 92–93

Fleetwood, Sara Iredell, 92–93

Ford's Theater, 35, 43, *44*, 44–45

Forten, James, 70

Fortune, T. Thomas, 88

Franklin and Armfield Slave Dealers, 18–20; Freedom House Museum, 18

Freedman's Hospital, 93

Freedman's Savings Bank/Freedman's Savings and Trust Company, *36, 36–37*, 93
Freedom Plaza, 43
Frelinghuysen University, 96
Fuller, Margaret, 24
Furgurson, Ernest B., 133; *Freedom Rising*, 133–34

Gallatin, Albert, 123
Gallaudet, Edward, 134
Garfield, James A., 123
Garnet, Henry Highland, 184
Garnet-Patterson Junior High School, 184–85, 202
Gatewood, Willard B., 70, 84–85; *Aristocrats of Color*, 70, 84–85
Gath (George Alfred Townsend), 5, 42, 146
Gaye, Marvin, 184
Gelderman, Carol, 101; *A Free Man of Color and His Hotel*, 101
Gilman, Daniel Coit, 134
Glyndon, Howard (Laura Redden Searing), 4–5
Gobright, Lawrence A., 4, 42
Goode, George Brown, 63
Grant, Henry, 173
Grant, Ulysses S., 33, 35, 70
Greeley, Horace, 24
Griffith Stadium, 82
Grimké, Angelina Weld, 70, 170, 182
Grimké, Archibald H., 70, 182
Grimké, Charlotte Forten, 4, 68–72, *69*, 182; "The Gathering of the Grand Army," 71–72
Grimké, Francis James, 68
Grimké Elementary School, 181–82
Gurdjieff, George Ivanovich, 202

Harlan, James, 50
Harris, Clara, 35
Hatton, Isaiah T., 80, 176; Dunbar Theater/Southern Aid Society, 78–80; Whitelaw Hotel and Apartments, 176–77

Hay, John, 4, 123, 124–26, 128–29, 130, 133, 136, 140, 141, 145; correspondence, 129, 145
Hay-Adams Hotel, 130–33
Hayes, Rutherford B., 123, 139
Hearst, William Randolph, 150
Hemenway, Robert, 206; *Zora Neale Hurston*, 206
Henderson, Archibald, 21
Henry, Joseph, 63
Henson, Josiah, 4
Hiawatha Theater, 187–88
Hillsdale Pioneer Association, 64
Hillsdale School, 65
Hines, Earl "Fatha," 177
Holiday, Billie, 169
Honey, Maureen, 195; *Aphrodite's Daughters*, 195–96
Horne, Lena, 80
hotels: Dunbar Hotel, 79; Hay-Adams Hotel, 130–33; Whitelaw Hotel and Apartments, *176*, 176–77; Willard Hotel/Willard's/Willard Inter-Continental, *41*, 41; Wormley Hotel, 124–26
Howard T. Mackey National Courts Building, 134–38, *135*
Howard Theater, 80–81, *81*, 185
Howard, Thomas, Sr., 17
Howard University, 5, 70, 80, 82, 84, 85–86, 93, 94–95, 97–98, 106, 159, 165, 168, 170, 171, 174, 175, 177, 178, 179, 180, 184, 186, 203–4
Howe, Julia Ward, 41
Hughes, Langston, 5, *158*, 159–91; *The Big Sea*, 166–67, 171, 174, 192
Hull, Gloria T., 78, 86; *Color, Sex and Poetry*, 86–87, 196; *Give Us Each Day*, 78
Hull, Isaac, 19
Hull, Joseph, 19
Huntington, Collis P., 150
Hurston, Zora Neale, 5, 159, 165, 170, 177, 186, 196, 203–8, *204*; correspondence, 205, 206, 207; "How It Feels to Be Colored

Me," 207–8; *Their Eyes Were Watching God,* 205

Industrial Bank, 64, 187–88
Ingersoll, Robert, 34, 91, 137
Israel Bethel Colored Methodist Episcopal Church, 17–18, 65

Jackson, Andrew, 22, 33–34, 133–34, 139
Jackson, Helen Hunt, 24
James, Henry, 132
Jennings, Paul, 4
Johnson, Andrew, 35, 70
Johnson, Georgia Douglas, 78, 169–72, *170,* 181, 183, 192–97, *193,* 206; *Bronze,* 194; "Common Dust," 197; correspondence, 192, 195, 196–97; "The Heart of a Woman," 197
Johnson, James Weldon, 5, 187, 190; "To America," 190–91
Journal of Negro History, 165
Jungle Inn/Music Box, 164, 185
Just, Ernest E., 85–86
Just, Ethel Highwarden, 85–86

Keckley, Elizabeth, 5
Kemble, Fanny, 24
Key, Francis Scott, 4, 13–16, *14,* 21; "Defense of Fort M'Henry," 15–16; "To My Cousin Mary," 16
Key Elementary School, 15
King, Clarence, 123, 124–26, 134; as James Todd, 125
King, Martin Luther, Jr., 189

La Farge, John, 144
Lafayette, Marquis de (Gilbert du Motier), 133
Lafayette Park/Lafayette Square, *33,* 33–35, 119, 123, 133–34, 136, 138, 140, 205
Lafayette Square Opera House, 136–38, *137;* as Belasco Theater, *137,* 138; as Stage Door Canteen, 138
Langley, Samuel P., 63

Langston, John Mercer, 168
Lankford, John A., 188; True Reformers Hall, 173, 188
Larsen, Nella, 174
Latrobe, Benjamin Henry, 126
L'Enfant, Pierre, 43
Lewis, John Whitelaw, 176; Whitelaw Hotel and Apartments, *176,* 176–77
Lewis, Sinclair, 5, 198–201, *199; Babbitt,* 198; *Main Street,* 198–201
Library of Congress, 18, 78, 86, 90–91
Lincoln, Abraham, 5, 29, 33–35, 43, 44–45, 49, 67, 119, 126, 128, 130, 141
Lincoln Colonnade, 162
Lincoln Theater, 162, *163*
Literary Lovers, 184
Locke, Alain, 162, 170, 174; *The New Negro,* 162
Lomax, Alan, 164
Louis, Joe, 176
Luria, Sarah, 133; *Capital Speculations* 133
Lynch, John R., 84

M Street High School/Dunbar High School, 5, 79, 96, 97, 159, 165, 173–74, 181, 182, 183, 202
Mabley, "Moms," 80
Madison, Dolley, 134, *135*
Mayfair Mansions Apartments, 186
McGill, James H., 82, 95
McHenry, Elizabeth, 193; *Forgotten Readers,* 193–94
McKay, Claude, 174
McKinley, William, 130, 139
Menard, John Willis, 4
Mencken, H. L., 198
Mesrobian, Mihran, 133
Metropolitan African Methodist Episcopal Church, 18
Metropolitan Club, 141
Meyer, Annie Nathan, 207
Miller, Kelly, 5, 170, 174–75, 203

Miller, May, 170, 203

Mills, Clark, 34

Mills, Cynthia, 145; *Beyond Grief,* 145

Minnehaha Theater, 163

Mix, Charles E., 49–50

Monday Night Literary Society, 90

Moore, Jacqueline M., 80, 98; *Leading the Race,* 80, 98–99

Morris, Roy, Jr., 48; *The Better Angel,* 48

Morse, Samuel F. B., 63

Morton, "Jelly Roll," 164

Mt. Olivet Cemetery, 15

Murray, Daniel Alexander Payne, 91, 101

Murray's Palace Casino, 183–84, 188

Music Box/Jungle Inn, 164

Mu-So-Lit Club, 184

National Association of College Women, 94, 98

National Association of Colored Women, 69

National Association of Colored Women's Clubs, 98

National Association for the Advancement of Colored People (NAACP), 98, 174, 184, 186–87

National Geographic Society, 135, 137

National Press Club, 42

National Statuary Hall, 107

National Theater, 43, 137

Nelson, Robert J., 100, 183

Newman, Arthur C., 83

New National Era, 106

New Negro, The, 162

Newspaper Row, 42

newspapers and journals: *Crisis,* 174, 187; *Fire!!,* 205; *Journal of Negro History,* 165; *New National Era,* 106; *North American Review,* 122; *Opportunity,* 175; *Washington Bee,* 67; *Washington Eagle,* 78, 182–83; *Washington Sentinel,* 168

New York Avenue Presbyterian Church, 34

Nicolay, John George, 130, 141

North American Review, 122

Nugent, Richard Bruce, 170, 177, 191, 205; "Shadow," 191

Oak Hill Cemetery, 95

O'Connor, William Douglas, 4

Omega Psi Phi fraternity, 86

Opportunity, 174, 175

O'Toole, Patricia, 126; *The Five of Hearts,* 126

Paine, Frederick H., 128

Paine, Lewis, 35

Painter, Uriah H., 136

Patent Office Hospital, 45–46, *46,* 49

Patterson, James, 184

Pen and Pencil Club, 90

Pendleton, Robert L., 164–65; Pendleton's High Grade Book and Job Printing, 164–65

Phelps Colored Vocational School, 181

Phoenix Inn, 188

Phyllis Wheatley YWCA, 186

Piatt, John James, 4

Piatt, Sarah Morgan Bryan, 4

Pinchback, P. B. S., 166, 202

Pittman, W. Sidney, 178; Twelfth Street YMCA, 178–79, *179*

Poe, Edgar Allen, 24

Pool, Rosey E., 196; *Beyond the Blues,* 196

Poore, Benjamin Perley, 42

Powell, John Wesley, 134

Powers, Hiram, 140; *The Greek Slave,* 140

Price, Kenneth M., 50

Prince Hall Masonic Temple, *185,* 185–86

public schools: Armstrong Technical High School/ Armstrong Manual Training School, 83, 182, 165; Burroughs Elementary School, 56;

Garnet-Patterson Junior High School, 184–85, 202; Grimké Elementary School, 181–82; Hillsdale School, 65; Key Elementary School, 15; M Street High School/Dunbar High School, 5, 79, 96, 97, 159, 165, 173–74, 181, 183, 202; Phelps Colored Vocational School, 181; Slowe Elementary School, 94; Sumner High School, 68

Pumphrey, Levy, 19

Pumphrey, William, 17

Ramsdell, Hiram J., 42, 146–48

Randolph, John, 128

Rathbone, Henry Reed, 35

Republic Gardens, 185, 188

Richardson, H. H., 130–32; Hay Mansion, Adams House, *130*, 130–32

Riggs, George, 141

Rock Creek Church Cemetery, 143–45, *144*

Rock Creek Park, 56–59, 122; Piney Branch, 58

Rockefeller, John D., 178

Roosevelt, Franklin D., 130, 139, 181

Roosevelt, Theodore, 128, 178

Saint-Gaudens, Augustus, 143–45; Adams Monument, 143–45, *144*

Samuels, Ernest, 139; *Henry Adams,* 139–40

Sandburg, Carl, 206

Schaffner, M. A., 150; "A Good Opinion of Bierce," 150–51

Schorer, Mark, 198

sculptures and monuments: Adams Monument (Augustus Saint-Gaudens), 143–45, *144;* Andrew Jackson Sculpture, Lafayette Park (Clark Mills), *33,* 33–35, 133–34; Emancipation Monument (Thomas Ball), 64; *The Greek Slave* (Hiram Powers), 140; National Statuary Hall, 107; Washington Monument, 39–40

Scurlock, Addison, 177–78, 188; Scurlock Photographic Studio, 177, 188

Seldon, Cary, 19

Seward, William, 34–35

Sharp, John G., 18

Shepherd, Alexander "Boss," 141

Sherman, William Tecumseh, 136, 141, 143

Shiner, Michael G., 17–22; *The Diary of Michael G. Shiner,* 18–20, *20–21*

Simmons, William J., 59–61, 65; *Men of Mark,* 59

Slayton Lyceum Bureau, 98

Slowe, Lucy Diggs, 94–95

Slowe Elementary School, 94

Slowe Hall, 94–95

Smith, Bessie, 205

Smithsonian Institution, 3, 45–47, *46,* 59, 61–63, 67, 124, 134, 140, 178

Snow, Beverly, 21–22; Epicurean Eating House, 21–22

Snow Storm (riot), 20–22

Southern Aid Society, 78–80

Stearns, Amanda Akin, 4

Stewart, William Morris, 146

Stillson, Jerome B., 42, 146

St. John's Episcopal Church, 34, 126–27, *127*

Stowe, Harriet Beecher, 4

Sumner, Charles, 141

Sumner High School, 68

Swinton, William, 42

Taft, William Howard, 171

Taylor, Billy, 184

Taylor, Elizabeth Dowling, 101; *The Original Black Elite,* 91, 101

Taylor, Zachary, 139

Terrell, Mary Church, 5, 88, 97–99; *A Colored Woman in a White World,* 88, 99

Terrell, Robert, 84–85, 97–98

theaters: Dunbar Theater, 78–80, *79;* Ford's Theater, 35, 43, *44,* 44–45; Hiawatha Theater, 187–88; Howard Theater, 80–81, *81, 185;* Lafayette Square Opera House, 136–38, *137;* Lincoln Theater, 162, *163;* Minnehaha Theater, 163; National Theater, 43, 137

Thoreau, Henry David, 55

Thornton, Anna Maria, 20–22

Thornton, William, 20

Thurman, Wallace, 177, 205

Tibbs, Roy W., 180

Tibbs, Thurlow, Jr., 181; Evans-Tibbs Collection, 181

Toomer, Jean, 166, 167, 170, 171, 201–3, 205; *Cane,* 167–68, 201–3

Traubel, Horace, 40

Tree, Lambert, 61

True Reformers Hall, 173, 188

Turf Club, 188

Turner, Darwin T., 201

Tuskegee Institute, 186, 205

Twain, Mark (Samuel Langhorne Clemens), 42, 146–49, *147; The Gilded Age,* 146, 148–49

Twelfth Street YMCA, 178–79, *179;* as Thurgood Marshall Center for Service and Heritage, 178–79, *179*

Union Seminary, 22

U.S. Capitol, 6, 20, 26, 40, 45, 57, 59, 91, 106, 107–8, 113, 143, 148–49, 167

U.S. Chamber of Commerce, 128–29

U.S. Geological Survey, 124

U.S. Patent Office, 45–46, *46,* 49–50, 124

U.S. Treasury, 36–37, *37–38,* 39, 43, 56–57, 68, 97, 123, *137,* 149

Vaughn, Sarah, 80

Ventura, Charlie, 169

Wadsworth, Alice Hay, 133

Walker, Alice, 207

Walker, James E., 83–84

Wardman, Henry, 133

Warner, Charles Dudley, 148

Washington Bee, 67

Washington City Orphan Asylum, 172

Washington Eagle, 78, 182–83

Washington Monument, 39–40

Washington Navy Yard, 17–20, 21

Washington Sentinel, 168

Webster, Daniel, 4, 24, 134; "Webster" (Botta), 24–26

Weitzman, Steven, 107

Wells, Gideon, 128

Wells, Virginia, 42, 146

White, George H., 84

White, Sanford, 145

White House, 4, 32–33, *33,* 40, 43, 45, 56, 61, 67, 70, 115, 131, 133, 138–39, 181

Whitelaw Hotel and Apartments, *176,* 176–77

Whitman, George, 29, 32

Whitman, Walt, 4, *28,* 29–53, 54–56, 91; correspondence, 33, 37–38, 39, 46, 47, 49; journalism, 49–50; in *New York Herald,* 48; notebooks, 38–39, 47; *Specimen Days,* 32, 41, 43, 45–46, 49, 50; "When I Heard at the Close of the Day," 51; "The Wound Dresser," 47; "Vigil Strange I Kept on the Field One Night," 52–53

Wilkes, Charles, 141

Willard Hotel/Willard's/Willard InterContinental, *41,* 41

Williams, Edward Christopher, 183–84

Wills, Garry, 142

Wilson, Woodrow, 139

Woodson, Carter G., 164–65, 170

Woolsey, Jane Stuart, 4

Wordsworth, William, 55

Wormley Hotel, 124–26

Wylie, Elinor, 152–55; "Wild Peaches," 153–55